INFORMATION BROKERING

A How-To-Do-It Manual

Florence M. Mason
Chris Dobson

**HOW-TO-DO-IT MANUALS
FOR LIBRARIANS**

NUMBER 86

NEAL-SCHUMAN PUBLISHERS, INC.
New York, London

Published by Neal-Schuman Publishers, Inc.
100 Varick Street
New York, NY 10013

Printed and bound in the United States of America.

Library of Congress Catalog Record Number 98–12371

ISBN 1–55570–342–9

CONTENTS

FIGURES

PREFACE

Today's explosion in information resources and new technology is opening up opportunities for individuals to build businesses that provide and manage information. All sorts of endeavors have come to be known by the term "information brokering." Individuals with experience in research, library science, writing, or specific industries can develop viable businesses that focus on some aspect of information. Starting a business is exciting, but it is also a bit frightening. As two women who jumped out of the ranks of the employed to start their own business—Chris in information brokering and Florence in consulting—we saw a need to develop a hands-on guide to help others who want to start up their own businesses. Chris has counseled many individuals on how to start up their own businesses. Materials that she developed for counseling and teaching adult education are the foundation of this book.

Florence's firm specializes in library management consulting. It was her teaching of master's-level courses in information brokering and information service design that sparked her interest in developing a basic guide to starting a successful small business.

It takes more than good searching skills to be an effective information broker. It also takes management skills. There are excellent books with detailed advice on searching for information, but we think there is also a need for a book that relates the basics of starting a small business to providing information.

This hands-on guide will help you to:

- understand what it takes to establish and operate a small business
- focus, develop, and market your information services business
- find sources and resources to guide your start-up.

Part I gives an overview of the information-brokering business for those who are just beginning to think about venturing out on their own. Chapter 1 discusses the skills, aptitudes, and knowledge you will need and how they all contribute to your business. We also provide a self-assessment tool to assist in diagnosing your own abilities and aptitudes. In Chapter 2, we help you analyze the market potential for a business niche and determine what products or services you will provide.

Based on our observations (admittedly limited), most entrepreneurs do not fail because they lack the talent to produce the product or service. Rather, they are tripped up by some aspect of self-employment that is only marginally related to the business they are in. Some have unreasonable income expectations or think that "setting your own hours" means working less rather than more. Others are just not aware of all that being self-employed entails. They may have become information brokers because they love doing research, but they find that they hate some of the tasks essential to staying in business, such as marketing and bookkeeping.

Parts II and III assume that you already have the skills to provide a valuable service and address the other aspects of an information-brokering business that are critical to staying in business. Part II offers practical advice on starting your information-brokering business. Chapter 3 discusses basics, such as forming your own corporation and organizing your office. Chapter 4 reviews bookkeeping, finances, and the important role played by key advisors, and Chapter 5 covers the all-important money matters such as setting fees and billing for services.

Part III moves into clients and marketing. Chapter 6 goes over working with your clients and getting them to pay for your services, and Chapter 7 helps you define a market niche and discusses ways to market your services. Finally, Chapter 8 looks at what it takes to be a responsible small business owner and how to avoid the pitfalls of conflict of interest and other problems that may ensnare a broker who is not fully aware of the ethics and subtleties of selling services.

At the end of each chapter there are recommendations for organizational and other resources that can help in your business start-up. The appendices supply additional references, including sources for federal and state tax regulations and business start-up, recommended books and articles for further reading, and codes of ethics from professional organizations.

You will find that, unlike some other books about information brokering, we do not focus on types of databases to search or techniques for doing searches. We think it most important instead that you learn, earn, or acquire the technical skills we cover before you contemplate going into business on your own. Information brokering is not a business for novices or for those right out of a master's program in library and information science. We firmly believe that if you want to start your own business, you should first gain experience and learn your techniques while working for an organization. Once you have these down, then you can strike out on your own. Learning how to operate and "grow" a business is enough of a challenge without having to learn how to produce the product at the same time.

Being an information broker can be immensely rewarding. As your business grows, you will have an increasing number of clients who look to you for your expertise and think of you as a critical element in the success of their businesses. Eventually you may even have the satisfaction of providing employment to other talented people. You have the ability to take advantage of opportunities and to guide your enterprise in whatever direction you wish. You also have a responsibility to your staff and your customers to make the right decisions. Our hope is that this book will help prepare you for both the opportunities and the responsibilities you will face as an entrepreneur.

Florence M. Mason
Chris Dobson

PART I

THE INFORMATION-BROKERING BUSINESS

1 BECOMING AN INFORMATION BROKER

BACKGROUND

Prior to 1969, when the term "information broker" starts to appear in the literature, the independent, profit-making business of selling information was grouped with other types of "information on demand" businesses. By the early 1970s, the business of private information provider had grown to a $10 million annual industry, and was predicted to grow tenfold during the next ten years (Garvin 1974).

Our discussions in this book concentrate on the information services sector commonly referred to as "information brokering." A broker, as defined by *Webster's*, is "a person paid a fee or commission for acting as an agent in making contracts or sales." Information brokers are a small subset of the information services business sector that encompasses database providers, primary market research firms, and even Internet service providers. Generically, information brokers locate, retrieve, manage, and/or organize information for clients. A sign of the industry's rapid expansion is in the growth of their professional organization, the Association of Independent Information Professionals (AIIP). Founded in 1986 with just twenty-nine members, by 1997 the association had grown to a membership of 864 members, 341 of whom were "regular members"— those who work full-time as information brokers.

Information brokers typically provide the following types of business services: research services—searching for information for individuals and organizations; information handling services—providing services to libraries, such as cataloging, filing, etc.; and other services—such as contracting, consulting, and publishing services provided to individuals and organizations. As we will discuss in later chapters, one of your first business start-up tasks should be to define carefully which specialty services you will offer. Once you have selected a service focus, your next step is to define the specific types of services you will offer, the techniques you will use in providing services, and the potential clients.

THE PROS AND CONS OF INFORMATION BROKERING

Before you set up your business, learn more about what information brokering is—and what it is not. First, the bad news. Despite what you may have read or believe to be true, being in the information services business is not a license to print money. The people who are successful information brokers do it because they really enjoy it, but it's a tough business, it's hard work, and there are only a few firms that have grown large enough to handsomely support their founders.

An information brokerage is usually a small business. Be aware that a large percentage of small business start-ups in the United States fail—57,000 each year. Starting a business involves considerable risk to your standard of living. While threats of downsizing may make employees nervous, self-employment is genuinely insecure. Unless you have an inheritance, a winning lottery ticket, or a spouse with a high-paying, secure job, the most dramatic change self-employment brings is a loss of financial security.

Your earnings and income may depend upon factors outside of your control, no matter how effective your marketing and selling skills. If your region or the local industry is in an economic downturn, it will be very difficult to generate new business. Even in boom times, growing an information business is a slow process. For the first three to five years, the amount you will be able to pay yourself may vary. If living with financial uncertainty is not for you, self-employment may not be your best choice.

There are, however, equally good reasons to consider becoming an information broker. Although self-employment may bring financial insecurity, it also provides independence. As your own boss you can take control, make decisions, implement plans, and guide your business in the direction you want it to go. You answer to your clients, but not to a boss who does not understand your contribution to the company.

Even though you may work alone, expect to continue to have frequent contact with people. Although you may not meet your clients face-to-face, it is possible to develop satisfying relationships over the telephone. If you do telephone research, you will "meet" hundreds of people and cultivate key sources of information.

Above all, being an information broker is a continuing challenge. It is hard work to understand a client's business and his or her information needs. Locating a key piece of information is similar to solving a puzzle. Since business, technology, and sources are always changing, there is an opportunity to learn new things every day. The intellectual satisfaction of providing the client with exactly the right information is very rewarding.

IDENTIFYING AND ACQUIRING THE RIGHT SKILLS

You need to consider whether you have the determination along with the necessary aptitudes and skills to be successful in this work. Owning one's own business can be exciting and rewarding, but succeeding as an entrepreneur requires more than talent and a bright idea. It also requires sacrifice and enormous amounts of hard work. Before setting your foot on the path to self-employment, it is essential that you conduct a serious self-analysis.

Crucial to your success is whether you possess the skills and ability to manage a business. Most people possess greater ability or aptitude in certain skill areas than in others. Skills are also intertwined with personality and attitude, and that makes developing them in some areas difficult. Management studies show, however, that people can improve their performance and overall effectiveness through practice and training. Take some time to assess your basic personality and aptitudes, and you will be better able to determine whether you can develop all the skills necessary to succeed as an information broker. If some skills seem too difficult or onerous, then decide whether or not they are essential to your success, and if so, if you are willing to acquire them anyway.

The management literature shows that there are three categories of developable skills; these skills are equally important if you want to operate a business successfully. You need: interpersonal skills, the ability to work with people; conceptual skills, the ability to acquire, process, and disseminate information effectively; and technical skills, an understanding of, and proficiency in the methods, processes, procedures, and techniques in a given area (Katz 1974). Any task, from online searching to talking to strangers, becomes easier with practice. If, however, you must learn a number of new skills and dramatically change your way of working and thinking, you need to evaluate carefully whether you are willing to accept the challenge.

Skills comprise your ability to translate knowledge into action. Do not overlook conducting a self-assessment of your own skills in order to determine whether information work will be a good fit for your talents and abilities. If you find you have strengths in a particular area, then capitalize upon these; if there are weaknesses, develop a strategy for strengthening your skills in this area. Figure 1–1 (page 10) gives a brief tool to help you define your entrepreneurial potential.

INTERPERSONAL SKILLS

Having good interpersonal skills means you are able to work effectively with other people, that you cannot only understand the needs of others but also motivate them. Self-awareness and a sensitivity to human relationships along with the ability to build relationships and contacts with people are essential in building a successful business.

Motivation

Self-motivation is important, as is the ability to motivate others. Generally, motivation in this field has little connection with a desire for wealth. True, most information brokers wish to make a comfortable living, but they are motivated more by the enjoyment they derive from the job, for without that, it is difficult, if not impossible, to succeed. So, expect to derive pleasure from performing the work, not from the results—because, although satisfied, few clients will verbally express their satisfaction. They take a well-performed job for granted; that is why they pay you.

It also helps to possess enormous curiosity and the capacity to derive pleasure from learning new things. Without the enthusiasm and energy that come from doing what you love, you will be an unconvincing salesperson and have difficulty providing your services. So be passionate and take great pride in your work, and find ways to motivate yourself to do those tasks you really do not enjoy. Cold calling and balancing the checkbook have to be done, and there may not be anyone to whom you can delegate the work. If your business provides a terrific service but you never get around to sending out invoices, your business will fail.

Salesmanship

As the founder of a small business, you are not only in charge of production, but you are also the primary salesperson. Even if your business is able to employ others to make the initial contacts with prospective clients, you are the one who must close the sale. Since all the varieties of information brokering are essentially personal services, you need to sell the benefits of your service and to sell yourself.

Selling requires the ability to talk confidently to people whom you don't know. It also requires the ability to accept rejection without personal distress. Disappointment is normal when a potential client decides not to engage your services, but do not take it as a reflection of your abilities or your worth as a person. There are always many more rejections than sales. Consider attending seminars on sales techniques if you have never been involved in sales. Even though your business may fly without you utilizing some of the more aggressive sales techniques such as cold calls, you must be able to close a sale and to make sure the client pays for services received.

CONCEPTUAL SKILLS

You need conceptual skills to receive and transmit information effectively. These are involved in making decisions about work schedules and strategies, handling problems effectively, and negotiating with clients. An information broker depends upon interviewing both clients and sources, so develop the ability to ask pointed and clarifying questions and learn to accurately interpret and record the responses. These critical skills will enable you to elicit the information you need from your client. Librarians train in the technique of conducting a reference interview, which breaks down the interview between a client and the librarian into a series of discrete activities. If you are not already trained as a librarian or information professional, become familiar with these techniques. There are many skills-building courses, ranging from improving interpersonal communication to honing listening and interviewing skills. Look for these courses through your local community college, business programs, or independent seminars.

An information broker must write clearly, use proper grammar, and spell correctly, be it for an introductory letter to a prospect, summarizing the results of a research project, or delivering recommendations to a consulting client. Take advantage of the spell checker and grammar checker programs available as part of word processing packages and as stand-alone programs. If you have significant difficulty with grammar or with expressing yourself clearly in writing, take a course at a community college in developmental or business writing. Effective writing is primarily the result of thinking carefully about what you want to say. A course can help you develop a personal writing style that is easy to read and actually says what you intend.

The ability to be self-reliant and confident about your decisions is another important skill. If you are not a "follower," that is, if you prefer to rely on your own assessment of situations rather than seek the opinions of others, you may be well-suited to become an independent small business owner. Even so, individuals who go to work for themselves say that one of the most difficult aspects of self-employment is the loss of the support of colleagues and coworkers. As an owner of a small, independent business, expect to work alone or with just one other person. There may not be other people around to serve as a sounding board when making decisions, and you will have a lot of decisions to make. Colleagues met through professional associations, such as the Association of Independent Information Professionals, can be very helpful and can become good friends. But such colleagues do little to relieve the solitude of working entirely by yourself.

Be organized. One of the consequences of self-employment is a loss of the routine organizing structure of a larger business or organization. The familiar pattern of meetings, lunch hours, and report deadlines that you might be accustomed to in your previous job will disappear, as will the routines of particular job functions. If you are constrained by the traditional work environment, self-employment may be liberating, but if you need a structured environment, the loss of organization can be paralyzing. As an entrepreneur, you must develop your own job description and routine to encompass every facet of your business, from accounting to shipping. So organize your office for efficient operation; a small business cannot afford inadequate filing systems, delays in billing, or project delays. Remember that the time spent trying to find a vendor's invoice is time you cannot bill to a client. Although courses are available on setting up accounting and even organizing closets, if you are chronically disorganized or a procrastinator, self-employment may not be a good career choice.

TECHNICAL SKILLS

Technical skills for information brokers encompass information-handling skills associated with diagnosing information needs of clients, identifying information sources, searching for information, and repackaging information in a manner appropriate for clients. Many information brokers rely on the skills they have developed through prior work experience—those who provide online searching, for instance, often have worked as corporate librarians and learned their skills on the job. Technical skills can be learned if you have the aptitude. However, if you are not basing your business on skills already learned, you should analyze the characteristics common to those who have them. For instance, expert online searchers must be able to make decisions quickly, remember the details of database content and format peculiarities, and comprehend what they read. Catalogers and indexers must be able to analyze written material quickly, and to accurately identify the primary focus and conclusions of a document. Training is available for most of the technical skills used by information professionals, but you must have the appropriate personality traits for the training to be effective. If you are not sure exactly what is involved in providing a particular service, ask other information brokers what they consider to be critical aptitudes.

Focus on a particular subject area in which you already have significant knowledge. If you have limited experience as a researcher but detailed knowledge of a particular industry, design your services to provide guidance to clients on the kind of information they can expect to receive even if you cannot discuss particular databases. Without either specialized skills or subject expertise, your learning curve may be intolerably steep.

You do not need to be a computer programmer to be an information broker, but you do need to be able to follow installation instructions, perform minor troubleshooting, and operate the software. If you need them, take courses to learn the basics of Microsoft Windows and other popular word processing, spreadsheet, and database management packages. If you are uncomfortable with a computer, however, you would be wise to first go through the tutorial that comes with your requisite software packages before you take a course. Use the software for a few weeks, and then take the course again, if necessary.

A PROFILE OF THE INFORMATION BROKER

ABILITIES	EDUCATION
Logical	Information Skills
Communicative	Knowledge of: 　Systems 　Vendors 　Sources
Energetic	Computing Skills
Self-Confident	Search Engine Skills
Decisive	Subject Knowledge
	Interview and Client Skills

Figure 1-1   Self-Assessment Guide for the Potential Entrepreneur

The transition from employee to entrepreneur involves a real change in work environment. The following short self-assessment tool can help you analyze your ability to cope with these changes. If the preponderance of your answers are Bs, self-employment may not be a sound career choice for you.

1. Do you prefer to work alone?

    A. _____ yes   B. _____ no

2. When making a decision, do you:

    A. _____ like to rely on your own assessment of a situation?
    B. _____ prefer to consult several others before making a decision?

3. When your ideas or suggestions are rejected, do you feel that:

    A. _____ you did not present them well?
    B. _____ those who rejected your ideas don't like you?

4. Do you need the approval or praise of a supervisor to motivate you?

    A. _____ yes   B. _____ no

5. Do you:

    A. _____ often think of ways to improve the way your department functions?
    B. _____ prefer to leave things the way they are and concentrate on doing your best?

6. Do you:

    A. _____ enjoy receiving unexpected rush assignments?
    B. _____ like to know exactly what you will be working on several days in advance?

7. When you attend a professional function do you:

    A. _____ make an effort to meet new people?
    B. _____ talk to the people you already know?

SOURCES

CITED IN TEXT

Garvin, Andrew. "Information on Demand." ASIS (American Society for Information Science) Annual Meeting Panel Discussion, October 15, 1974, Atlanta, Georgia.

Katz, Robert L. "Skills of an Effective Administrator." *Harvard Business Review* (September/October 1974): 23–35.

Webster's Dictionary of the English Language. Unabridged. 3rd ed., 1993, s.v. "broker."

FOR FURTHER INFORMATION

Burwell's Bibliography on Information Brokering, $25.00, is published semiannually.

The Burwell World Directory of Information Brokers. $99.50.

The Burwell Directory on Disk, $150.00.

All available from Burwell Enterprises, 3724 FM 1960 West, Suite 214, Houston, TX, 77068, phone: (251) 537-9051, fax: (251) 537-8332. www.burwellinc.com.

The Internet Directory of Express Library Services, published by FYI Information Services of the County of Los Angeles Public Library and Information Researchers, University of Illinois, an outgrowth of the *FISCAL Directory of Fee-Based Research and Information Services*, $75.00 (American Library Association 1996). The *Fiscal Directory* is available from American Library Association, Book Order Fulfillment, 155 N. Wacker Drive, Chicago, IL 60606–1719, phone 1-800-545-2433, press 7.

The Information Professional's Institute offers practical seminars on accessing information, and on establishing, managing, and marketing an information brokerage. $225.00. Operated by Sue Rugge and Helen Burwell. Contact the Information Professional's Institute at 3724 FM 1960 West, Suite 214, Houston, TX 77068, phone: (251) 537–8344, fax: (251) 537–8332.

Consider joining these professional associations:

Association of Independent Information Professionals (AIIP), 234 W. Delaware Ave., Pennington, NJ 08534; (609) 730–8749.

The Special Libraries Association (SLA), 1700 18th Street NW, Washington, DC 20009–2508, phone: (202) 234–4700; SLA has offered a course on information brokering at its June annual meeting since 1985.

Amelia Kassel runs a unique one-on-one mentoring program for persons who are interested in learning about the information-brokering field and its business practices. She also offers seminars on becoming an information broker. Her speciality areas are competitive intelligence, marketing research, and worldwide business information. Contact Ms. Kassel at (800) 544–5924, fax: (707) 823–2713, e-mail: mbase@ix. net.csn.com.

Library schools offer courses in online searching. For lists of accredited schools of library and information science, consult the *Bowker Annual*, available at your public library, or the American Library Association Web site: www.ala.org/alaorg/oa/schools.html.

Most of the online services such as Dialog or Dow Jones offer searching seminars whose prices range from free to fee. Contact the individual database producers for more information.

2 DEVELOPING YOUR SERVICE DELIVERY STRATEGY

We believe that if you are going to be a success as a small business, you need to focus on specific services. In other words, you need to develop an information broker "niche." *Webster's Dictionary* defines a niche as "a place or position particularly suitable for the person or thing in it." We define a niche as described by these three elements:

- the nature of the information you provide
- the techniques you use to obtain information
- the nature of your customers.

In some cases, your niche may be a combination of these elements. The more elements you use to define the niche, the narrower it will be. Picking a niche allows you to develop a distinct identity for your company, makes your marketing manageable, and allows you to focus on those activities you do best and enjoy most.

In choosing a niche, you must analyze three elements: your skills, the market, and what arouses your passion. As we discussed in Chapter 1, it is important that you examine your skills, aptitudes, and existing knowledge and determine how they fit with your business concept. But you also need to examine, define, and pursue a market (see Chapter 7), for if there is no demand or if the service is available from other sources for free, you will not be able to base a business on that service, no matter how skilled you are. To make it all work, you must be interested in and really enjoy your work. Starting a business requires long hours and great commitment. If you do not enjoy what you are doing, you are not likely to have the determination needed to make the business a success: information brokering works only for those who like to do it, and it is difficult to make a rational, cost-justified case for choosing this profession (Rugge and Glossbrenner 1992).

WHAT INFORMATION BROKERS DO

Information-brokering services focus primarily on accessing and delivering information in a customized manner to fit client needs. Build an identity for your company that is solid and uniform by focusing your services on a niche. You have a number of choices in selecting a niche (see Figure 2–1 [page 17] for some of the service specializations you might consider); your strongest opportunities may well come from new, emerging fields that could form the basis of a viable business. There are also service niches, such as competitive intelligence, which involves assembling information on business competitors, and personal data research, which involves public records searches. Each type of service requires different technical skills, involves different clients and information needs, and has distinct characteristics. Although this book is designed to help you begin a business focused on research services, it is important to include here a brief discussion of the additional information service niches so you are aware of them.

Selecting a niche limits the size of your potential market, but keep in mind that you are just one person. Most sales in the information business result from personal contacts with clients, and you can contact only so many people. Choosing a niche enables you to contact those who are the most likely prospects for what you have to offer. For example, if your market is not-for-profit watchdog groups, you should be able to identify your prospects with relative ease and to tailor all your marketing materials to address the specific needs of your prospects. Then you will be able to use a variety of marketing techniques repeatedly, without spending a fortune, because you will be addressing the same group of clients.

RESEARCH SERVICES

Most information brokers provide general or specialized research services to companies and individuals, and many offer other services as well. There are three basic ways information brokers locate information: by searching online databases, by searching manually through printed documents, and by calling experts. All three techniques require specialized skills and knowledge of sources. Research skills, whether online, manual, or telephone, are developed through use. If you do not have significant experience in doing research, you may want to subcontract some highly specialized work to more experienced information brokers until you are confident you can deliver a quality service to your clients.

Online searching is likely to be your most frequently used skill, and it has the most significant learning curve. Taking one class in online searching at a university or from a vendor does not make you an expert. As Mary Ellen Bates, owner of Bates Information Services and past president of the AIIP, observed, "You need to have an in-depth knowledge of research and information services—or be willing to subcontract the research—you cannot learn to do research on-the-job while self-employed" (LEXIS-NEXIS 1996).

ONLINE RESEARCH

Every information broker should have a strategy for using online sources when they are appropriate. In addition to knowing how to access the databases, the information broker will need to subscribe to the services or make arrangements for another information broker to do the searches. Online databases are electronic collections of information and may comprise an index to articles (like the *Reader's Guide to Periodical Literature*), a publication (like the *Wall Street Journal*), or a directory (like *Dun's Million Dollar Directory*). The database producer, usually a publisher, puts the information in machine-readable form and sells the tape to the online service. CompuServe, Prodigy, and NEXIS are all online services, and hundreds more are emerging with the pervasiveness of Internet access.

In many cases, publishers are even bypassing the online services and making their databases available directly through the Internet. The online service provides the search interface (ranging from esoteric command languages to easy-to-use forms), maintains the computers on which the databases reside, and performs the accounting functions related to use. To search a database, the end user directs his or her modem to dial a high-speed telecommunications network, such as Sprintnet, or an Internet service provider. The end user is then connected to the online service's computer through high-speed, long-distance lines. Even with the availability of direct access to these databases, end users will still seek the services of information brokers who use more sophisticated search engines than those usually available on free sites, have expertise in evaluating information and, above all, have the time to do a complete, high-quality search.

Some database services provide two user interfaces, one for novices and one for experts. Although the more friendly interfaces may seem easier to use, most sacrifice some search capability. Menu systems are slower to use and tend to deliver huge quantities of information that must be reviewed to identify relevant portions. Using a command language, expert searchers can locate quickly exactly the information they need.

Most information brokers involved in online research subscribe to Dialog, Inc., one of the oldest and largest online services. Dialog has over 530 databases covering an enormous range of subjects. Directories of businesses, abstracts of articles in technical publications, industry newsletters, market research reports, and newspapers are just a few of the types of documents included. Data-Star, a companion service to Dialog, provides exclusive access to many European business, scientific, and newspaper databases.

For those who do business research, newspapers are also an essential source. For complete coverage here, you need two other services: Dow Jones and LEXIS-NEXIS. In addition to having a large number of newspapers, wire services, and trade publications, Dow Jones is the only service to offer the text of the *Wall Street Journal*. The LEXIS-NEXIS service provides legal information as well as business and news sources, and subscribers can select a subset of the service. For those who need only the business and news capability, the NEXIS portion offers the full texts of domestic and international publications, market research and brokerage reports, and key reference material. LEXIS-NEXIS is the only service that provides significant retrospective access to the *New York Times* (from 1980 forward). More and more daily newspapers are becoming available through the Internet, but most lack the capability to search back issues. In addition, the commercial services allow you to search over fifty newspapers at once. If you are looking for articles from a particular region or nationwide, you need to be able to search multiple newspapers simultaneously.

According to the January 1997 *Gale Directory of Databases,* there are currently 879 online services providing access to 5,677 databases (see Appendix A for a list of the most popular database services). Costs for most online services are based on usage, and many also require an annual or monthly subscription fee. Subscription fees can amount to several thousand dollars if you subscribe to a number of services so the Association of Independent Information Professionals (AIIP) has negotiated with many vendors, including online services, to waive the fees for regular members. A significant advantage of selecting a subject niche is that you don't have to subscribe to a lot of online services in order to serve customers.

Once you have identified your niche, the *Gale Directory of Databases* and BiblioData's *Fulltext Sources Online* can be extremely useful in identifying the online services you will require. The *Gale Directory* provides descriptions of individual databases, indexed by subject, with the online services that supply access. *Fulltext Sources Online* lists individual publications and the online databases and services that include the publications. If you know the key publications and bibliographic resources for your niche industry, you should be able to identify the databases and online service that will provide access.

COMPACT DISCS

If you have a narrow specialization, owning one or more compact discs (CDs) may be a viable alternative to using the databases through an online service. In fact, some specialized resources may only be available on CD and not online. (The most reliable source of information

Figure 2–1 Information Services Business Specialties

1. Research services
    By technique
    telephone
    online
    By source
    public records
    patents
    government information
    By subject area
    medicine
    law
    chemistry
    environment
    donor research
    electronics
    pharmaceuticals
    import/export/international business
    competitive intelligence

2. Information handling
    document delivery
    book indexing
    thesaurus construction
    translating
    abstracting
    library services
    update filing
    cataloging

3. Contracting/consulting/publishing
    library staffing
    consulting
    grant preparation assistance
    information audits
    systems analysis and design
    training/seminars in information services
    writing
    articles
    books
    compiling/editing books
    technical writing

on the availability of a title on CD is the publisher.) Many CDs that contain research information range in cost from $1,000 to $8,000; most are annual subscriptions that generally include quarterly or monthly updates. One advantage of compact discs is that each CD is the equivalent of a complete online database. For example, one popular CD, *Computer Select*, has the text of over 200 computer-related magazines plus directories of hardware and software, and it is priced at less than $1,500. This may sound expensive, but remember that you pay for it once and can use it as much as you want. In addition, you can see your search results and refine your strategy without incurring additional charges. If you hit the wrong key it does not matter; you can spend as long as you need on the search.

The disadvantages of CDs are their comparatively high cost and long "lag time"— the period between publication of a document and its inclusion on the CD in hand. If your specialization is an area of dynamic information, you will still need to search online for the most recent four to eight weeks of data. If you expect to do a fair amount of high-tech research, you can easily justify the cost of the CD. Otherwise, online searching may be more cost-effective. For example, the indexing on *Computer Select* lags a month behind publication, and full text is not available in most cases for two months. If your client wants really recent computer news, you may still have to go online.

INTERNET SEARCHING

Aside from its function as a way to access online databases, the Internet is more useful as a communications capability than as a research tool. You can send messages and files to people all over the world if you know their e-mail addresses. However, an increasing amount of useful information is available on the Internet. You can download files that are available at individual locations from Web pages. You can use other computers at other locations—for instance, you can dial into more than 300 library catalogs through the Internet and view the contents of those library collections. You can also join bulletin board–type forums called "usenets." There is a usenet for every interest, and their use grows daily.

In general, however, with the Internet, you get what you pay for. Material on the Internet is whatever an individual, company, organization, or government agency chooses to make available. No one manages the Internet, although a few committees promulgate communication standards and operational suggestions. The result is just what you would expect. There are files of wonderful information somewhere on the Internet, virtually free, the same information you may pay to retrieve from a database vendor or reference book publisher. The trick is finding the information. Because no one controls the Internet, no one knows what or who is on it.

The advent of the World Wide Web and companies rushing to develop company Web pages means that you can now retrieve a variety of business-related materials over the Internet. In particular, you can readily find corporate press releases, annual reports, and product literature. Third-party analyses of a company's prospects, however, are not likely to be found on the Internet. The Internet has also dramatically increased the availability and ease of access to a wide variety of government documents and information.

The unmanaged nature of the Internet means that information brokers must supply sufficient information about where they found the information on the Internet so the client can properly evaluate its worth. The information broker cannot guarantee the accuracy of the data, but he or she can provide the author's name, affiliation, and the source and date of publication so the client can judge on the likely veracity of the information.

TELEPHONE RESEARCH

Telephone research may be an adjunct to online research or it may be a specialization. It requires a degree of charm, the ability to make people want to help you, patience in following a trail of leads, and superior note-taking ability. For information that is obscure or on the leading edge of a technology, telephone research may be the only option. Numerous organizations collect data that are never published or are buried in esoteric publications not indexed in online databases. In the case of late-breaking events or new technological developments, the articles have not even been written yet. A telephone researcher uses sources such as the *Encyclopedia of Associations* to identify organizations and individuals with an interest in a particular subject and then makes calls to locate the particular individual with the needed information. You need excellent interviewing skills to obtain comprehensive information from sources and must also balance the need to protect the confidentiality of the client with the responsibility of not violating the trust of the source. In talking with sources by telephone, the telephone researcher must also endeavor to establish that person's credentials—for example, degrees and publications should be verified.

MANUAL RESEARCH

Not everything is online. Certain kinds of research can only be done by hand. Some information is only available in reference books, or peculiarities of format required by the client make gathering the information manually much more cost effective than online retrieval. You can expect to use manual sources if you are looking for information on events before 1980. Although some bibliographic databases in the scientific/technical area cover publications before 1980, there are only a few with significant pre-1980 coverage in the business area e.g., IAC Promt, IAC Magazine Index, ABI/Inform.

Historical or trend research still requires using printed indexes and sources in paper or microform. So if your client needs information on pricing strategies for steel in 1975, get out your magnifying glass and head for the public library. Few newspapers were online before 1985, and much historical material currently is inaccessible online. Information brokers who specialize in manual research usually focus on a narrow subject niche. They are familiar with, and have convenient access to, certain specialized resources not available online.

Public records research often requires manual searching since online availability of public records varies with the jurisdiction. If you want to establish a business providing information for charities who are looking for donors, your work will likely involve manual searching. One broker manually searches divorce and real estate records to calculate the net worth of individuals and checks donor records published by universities and organizations such as museums. True, more information such as lawsuit, real estate, and bankruptcy records is becoming available online, but much of this material is still only available in print form.

Since manual searches require going to a library or public agency, be sure you have a thorough knowledge of the resources available in all the libraries within reasonable driving distance of your home or office before you set up shop. Spend time browsing the reference collections; really look at the reference books. Learn what is available in various sources, and find out what special resources the library has. If you cannot comfortably spend hours in a library, this is probably not the profession for you. Library research requires patience, a methodical approach, and an awareness that the clock is ticking. It's much like online searching in that you need to be resourceful in finding new avenues of research when one turns out to be a dead end. It also requires good eyes.

Get to know the librarians; they are wonderful, friendly, helpful people. They are also underpaid and overworked, so make your library visits during non-rush hours. In some areas librarians and information brokers have a difficult relationship. Do not ask the librarians to do your work, and don't monopolize either the personnel or the photocopy equipment at a public library. Be aware also that certain private university libraries may restrict your access or use because they are supported by student tuition fees and are organized to serve their university community.

PROVIDING NONRESEARCH SERVICES

As we mentioned earlier, you may wish to focus your business on offering specialized, nonresearch services. Some of these services provide document delivery or consulting or publishing services. Competitive intelligence has emerged as one of the hottest new services, and some information brokers blur the nature of their service by supplementing their information research services with public records and investigatory-type searching services.

DOCUMENT DELIVERY

Document delivery used to be one of the most basic and important services offered by information brokers, but advances in computer storage technology, computerized typesetting, scanning, and modem speeds have resulted in a dramatic increase in the number of publications online in full text, making the document delivery service obsolete for all but the most obscure materials. Although currently some charts and graphs are not online, within the next five years telecommunications technology will make transmission of graphics routine. Even if technology does not make this business obsolete overnight, the competition is fierce. Besides the established document delivery services, database producers will fax copies of documents. To be effective, a document delivery service must have convenient access to a large number of publications, reliable copy machines, and high-volume customers.

"INTRAPRENEURS," CONTRACTING, AND PUBLISHING

An emerging opportunity for information brokers is to become an intrapreneur, which involves setting up or running a fee-based information service business that is affiliated with a larger organization. A boon to public and academic libraries, a number of them—including the Los Angeles County Public Library, the Minneapolis Public Library, Purdue University, and Georgia Tech University—offer fee-based services as part of their organizational mission. These services try to cover the full cost of their operations, including overhead. Operating this kind of business offers the possibility of receiving a salary and benefits as part of a larger organization while operating a business focused on customers and customer satisfaction. FYI, the information brokerage at the Los Angeles County Library, is an example of a fee-based information brokerage operating within a library, but operated as a self-sustaining, fee-based business.

Publishing may be another attractive niche service to develop. Some information brokers have developed successful services in this area.

Burwell, Inc., a Houston-based, information-brokering company, offers a variety of published products, such as a directory of information brokers. Other brokers may offer newsletters or other specialized products.

Another business focus exists in contracting for services, in which you provide library management or information searching on a contract basis to private professional firms and businesses too small to retain the services of an information professional. Contract services may include supplying staff to the organization, purchasing and maintaining library collections of journals and monographs, filing loose-leaf services, and performing database searches and other services as specified. In this field, you would negotiate an annual contract with a client that would have a fixed price for the delivery of a set of specified services.

COMPETITIVE INTELLIGENCE

Some information brokers provide competitive intelligence (CI) services to their clients. Put simply, competitive intelligence involves researching and gathering information about companies to give a picture of an industry, a company, or a market segment (hence providing "intelligence"). Providing competitive intelligence services means interacting with a wide range of data sources, creatively finding and using alternative information sources and then gathering and sifting the data so it reveals a more understandable and possibly predictive pattern. The type of information sought by clients requires that the broker collect and organize both soft and hard data.

CI analysts act as "strategic advisors" who keep their business customers alert to the latest significant events about competitors in their industries. For instance a client may wish to know, "How will competitor A react if we push up the price of our product?" To answer this question, the broker may have to acquire both qualitative and quantitative data from a number of sources and then deduce an answer. CI work is more difficult than straightforward searching and research because certain kinds of data are not readily available. For example, a CI analyst may be asked to supply information on private or family-owned businesses, which are not subject to government regulation and thus very little public information exists about them. Or CI clients may seek current information that involves updating data from online sources on a regular basis or continuous monitoring of wire services and industry publications. Other CI activities may include analyzing a competitor's product (reverse engineering) or conducting telephone or in-person interviews with competitors' salespersons or employees.

Consider offering this type of service if you have specialized knowledge of an industry that you can leverage. Competitive intelligence skills include filtering great amounts of data, organizing and indexing information as relational databases, and employing methods of organizing and retrieving information. The skills relevant for competitive intelligence are taught in library science, information management, computer science, and records management courses. Brokers who offer CI services should be conscious that trouble may arise when clients push aggressively for activities that would require them to engage in inappropriate activities such as masquerading as a potential customer or paying for information obtained from a competitor's employees. Use of espionage tools such as untruthfulness, confidentiality breaches, eavesdropping, computer snooping, and similar techniques may be suggested explicitly or implicitly. Corporate intelligence gathering is legal and usually ethical; espionage for the most part is illegal and unethical as well. So long as brokers obtain information openly and with the informed knowledge of an employee or salesperson, competitive intelligence activities are legal and acceptable. Although the information broker should not reveal the client's name, sources contacted in the course of compiling competitive intelligence should be aware that the broker is conducting research for a third party.

Creative research approaches can be used to avoid problems of conducting CI types of research. Rather than asking direct questions such as, "What is X company's current marketing strategy?" the information broker may effectively determine the answer indirectly by finding out the number and type of service outlets it operates, changes in the size of the sales force, and the amount of and type of advertising currently being used by the firm. Sources for competitive intelligence include published company and industry data, government sources, contacts with research and development staff, editors and reporters of newspapers in the competitor's geographic area, editors of specialized industry newsletters, professional associations, suppliers and distributors, lobbying groups, and customers. Legal and ethical intelligence-gathering activities include obtaining published company reports, published sales and marketing data, SEC filings, ratings by industry agencies, and public records such as court records and government documents. Brokers may also collect and assess consultants' reports, market surveys, financial reports, and competitors' brochures. Knowledgeable researchers have also found that they can obtain information by using alternative sources such as industrial development authorities, chambers of commerce, industry newsletters, and newspaper sources in communities where the competitor has a major presence.

Competitive intelligence professionals have a professional organization, the Society for Competitive Intelligence Professionals (SCIP), which currently has more than 1,800 members. More information about competitive intelligence can be found in the Sources section at the end of this chapter and in the Basic Business Reference Sources after the appendices.

PERSONAL/PUBLIC-RECORDS RESEARCH, INVESTIGATORS

Another niche service provides information and research about persons through searches of public records sources. Be aware that the term "information broker" has been used in certain cases to describe services such as supplying investigatory searches. If you are interested in public-records searching, expect that your clients will ask you to gain access to and to search personal information files such as bank records, medical files, and court, public safety, police, and fire records. Working with personal data means you are involved in providing services that may include establishing financial qualifications of individuals, performing credit profiles, or be related to missing person traces, employee misconduct, computer crime, casualty losses, asset searches, fraud, legal issues, surveillance, and undercover work. In some states, if you provide personal searches or work with public records, you will be required to obtain a state license as an investigator. If you need to develop searching skills to search public records, consider taking courses in a journalism school that teaches techniques for investigatory reporters. Researchers who offer public-records-searching services have separate industry and professional groups.

SOURCES

CITED IN TEXT

Encyclopedia of Associations. Detroit: Gale, biennial.
Gale Directory of Databases, 2v. Detroit: Gale, semiannual.
LEXIS-NEXIS Information Professional Update, February 1996, p. 23.
Rugge, Sue, and Alfred Glossbrenner. *The Information Broker's Handbook.* New York: McGraw-Hill, 1992, xxi–xxiv.

Webster's Dictionary of the English Language. Encyclopedia ed., s.v. "niche."

FOR FURTHER INFORMATION

Society of Competitive Intelligence Professionals, 1700 Diagonal Road, Suite 520, Alexandria, VA 22314, phone: (703) 739–0696.

National Association of Investigative Specialists (NAIS), P.O. Box 33244, Austin, TX 78764, phone: (512) 719–3595, pimall.com

National Council of Investigative and Security Services (NCISS), P.O. Box 449, Severna Park, MD 21146, phone: (410) 647–3227.

Public Records Research, BRB Publications, Inc., 4653 South Lakeshore Drive, Suite 3, Tempe, AZ 85282, phone: (800) 929–3764, www.brbpub.com

ION Investigators Anywhere Resource Line. A newsletter for investigators that gives some insight into this business. 2111 East Baseline, Suite F7, Tempe, AZ 85283–1505, phone: (602) 730–8088.

Check newsletters such as *Information Report*, published by Washington Researchers, phone: (203) 333–3499; and *The Information Advisor*, published by FIND/SVP (212) 645–4500.

PART II
YOUR OWN BUSINESS

3 STARTING YOUR OWN FIRM

Once you have decided you have the passion and skills to be an information broker and have identified your niche, you are ready to set up your business. The biggest obstacle you are going to face is that the work is labor intensive and heavily dependent upon the skills of the entrepreneur and staff who operate the business. Planning is the key; if you fail to give your business a good foundation, you will have a hard time going back and taking these steps once you become busy with clients. Furthermore, establishing your business correctly from the beginning guards against mistakes that may cost time and money later on.

PREPARING A BUSINESS PLAN

Starting up a business involves a host of decisions: the type of business structure to adopt, how to organize an office, and what type of office equipment and software are needed. To assist in making these decisions, develop a business plan that helps you evaluate your business idea and communicate it to others. It is an invaluable way to think through the business or service you are planning to offer in a systematic and organized manner. On top of that, it is a useful vehicle that can inform others of your business idea. In addition, if you plan to borrow start-up capital, a business plan is a critical document to submit in soliciting loans.

It may seem that writing down a formal plan is taking you away from the exciting process of creating your business, but do not ignore this step. Plan well, and it is more likely your business will be a success. If you cannot articulate your services and convince others of their importance, then you are taking a risk in starting a new business at all.

You may wish to take a course on how to develop a business plan. Courses are available from universities and community colleges as well as from nonprofit centers that foster entrepreneurial and small business development. In addition to the discussion found here, consult the information on starting up a business in the Sources section at the end of this chapter.

A BUSINESS PLAN DEFINED

A business plan is more than just a template for a new business. It is a summary of your business idea. It should accurately describe your products or services as well as define customers and the competition. It should describe production methods and techniques, specify your general marketing approach, and discuss the management and financing of the business.

The business plan is a financial estimate and should supply an estimate of how much time and money will be required to start the business. If you plan to borrow money to start your business, most banks and financiers will expect you to provide a business plan as part of your request for financing.

The business plan is a dynamic document. It provides a course of action by which to achieve your goal—which is to start and operate a successful business. Think of starting a business as setting out on a trip; the business plan is your map. Expect that you will have to alter your route in response to changing conditions. Suppose you were about to set sail on a ship from Miami to Gibraltar. You would need a map and a route, an ocean-going ship with sails, and perhaps help in sailing the ship. To reach your destination, you would correctly set the course, set the sails, and then steer the ship according to ocean currents, winds, longitude, and latitude. The plan helps to ensure that you reach the goal.

WHAT DOES THE BUSINESS PLAN CONTAIN?

A basic business plan should answer these questions:

- What does the business do?
- Who are the customers?
- What are the services, and how are they defined?
- What are you going to do? Write your descriptions as action statements about what you intend to accomplish in your business.
- What is the value to your customers, and how much will they pay?

HOW LONG DOES IT TAKE TO PREPARE A BUSINESS PLAN?

Physically writing the business plan is only one part of the time commitment; thinking it through is what takes time. One estimate says it takes approximately thirty-five weeks to prepare a complete business plan from beginning to end (Brooks and Stevens 1987). The most time-consuming activities are assembling the detailed market description, which entails researching and knowing something about your market; preparing the plan, which is the physical writing task; presenting the plan, which may involve obtaining interviews with bankers if you are seeking capital funds for start-up; and preparing the definition of your products and services (see Figure 3–1 for an outline to get you started).

Figure 3–1 Business Plan Outline

Cover Page
    Name, principals, address, and telephone number

1. Business concept description
    A generic description would be to describe a service business that provides research services and products to clients through manual and computer services. This is your business focus or niche as described in Chapter 2.

2. Type of services
    Describe the services to be offered and the tools utilized
        Computers, hardware, and databases
        Other information on the business

3. Market and customers
    Need for the services
    Definition of the market and information about your market
    Expected penetration of the market
    Competition
    Pricing and sales of products

4. Business administration and management
    Personnel
    Form and structure of the business
    Other information

5. Financial data
    Sources of start-up funding
    Income projections—profit and loss
    Other information

6. Appendix
    Information to be included might be leases, letters of reference, brochures, contracts, or other pertinent documentation on the business.

FORMING THE BUSINESS STRUCTURE

One of the most important decisions in setting up your business is choosing the type of business structure. Obtain legal advice and inform yourself thoroughly regarding which one is right for your business. Since the tax code is constantly changing, make sure to obtain up-to-date information in this area before proceeding. In general, the most typical business structures are a sole proprietorship, a partnership, a general corporation, a Subchapter S corporation, and a limited liability company.

The *sole proprietorship* is the least complicated business form. There is one owner, and the business is not organized as a separate legal entity, as in the case of a corporation. All profits and losses are reported on the owner's personal income tax forms, using the IRS's Schedule C. Sole proprietors are directly responsible for liability and debt incurred by the business. The advantage of this form is that it is simple to set up and easy to organize. The least expensive, least complicated business structure, it is the best structure for the single owner working from home. There is no double taxation; you pay no corporate tax on your earnings. The disadvantage is that personal and business liability are mingled together with this form. With a sole proprietorship, the business entity does not survive the proprietor, which may be a concern if your spouse is involved in the business.

Consider establishing a *partnership* if your business will be owned and operated by two or more individuals. With this business structure, partners conduct business together and pool their collective capital; professionals such as attorneys, lawyers, and doctors commonly utilize this form. Partnerships are considered legal entities for the purpose of conveying real property, suing or being sued under the partnership name, and in bankruptcy procedures. You need a partnership agreement that defines the arrangements among the partners. It is a simple business form to create since there are no government requirements, but personal and business liability are not segregated. Partnerships do not offer perpetuity advantages, since partnerships do not survive the partner.

If there are two co-owners, be aware that the partnership form does not resolve the difficult dilemmas encountered if one partner is more involved in the business and wishes to receive more compensation. Partnerships can be a problem if one partner ends up doing 75 percent of the work, but the agreement states that profits are split evenly. Form a corporation to obtain more flexibility in adjusting contributions and compensation among owners.

When making the decision to form a partnership, make sure there is: (1) a good understanding with your partner about your roles in the business, (2) a prepared partnership agreement that spells out details of your relationship beyond the legal form, and (3) a dissolution clause in your agreement that spells out how to dissolve the partnership, if such a step becomes necessary. Dissolution is the single most difficult aspect of partnership agreements.

Forming a *general corporation* creates your business as a separate legal entity from your personal activities. In a corporation, the owners hold shares in the company. At a minimum, the corporation must have officers including a president and secretary/treasurer. Corporations must have "articles of incorporation," file applications with their state's secretary of state or corporation department for creation and dissolution, and follow state laws regarding record keeping and operation of the corporation. Corporations may be obligated to pay corporate filing fees, which may be nominal or range up to several hundred dollars. Corporations are stable and are perpetual and generally protect their owners from actions against them personally. Actions or suits for liabilities and debts are brought against the corporation and are the responsibility of the corporation, although there is still some uncertainty regarding professional negligence and malpractice protection (we discuss this in the liability section further on in this chapter). The disadvantages of this form are that corporations must be set up correctly, which can be time consuming, and they must follow government regulations in their operations. There are expenses for forming and maintaining a corporation, which include keeping a minutes book and filing annual corporate tax returns. Corporate taxation rules may also be disadvantageous to small owners. Check with your accountant on these matters before choosing a general corporation structure.

The *Subchapter S Corporation* is a special corporate form. The S-Corporation form establishes your business as a separate legal entity and has the advantages of a corporation, but your reporting and financial arrangements are less complicated, since profits and losses of the corporation are reported through the Schedule C form of the business owner's personal income tax return. Formerly, S-Corporations offered certain tax advantages, but the distinctions between a regular corporation and S-Corporation have lessened over time as a result of tax-reform legislation. Again, consult your accountant and attorney for advice about whether you should follow a general or S-Corporation form.

A *limited liability company (LLC)*, now available in most states, is formed when a group files an Article of Organization with the secretary of state and the members of the LLC execute an operating agreement. An LLC is more flexible than a limited partnership, since all members may be protected from debts of the entity under certain circumstances. It is also more flexible than an S-Corporation. In certain states, however, the LLC is not perpetual, which is a disadvantage.

REGISTERING THE BUSINESS NAME

Establishing your corporate image begins with the selection of a company name. The ideal name describes your business services and is memorable. Use a name rather than an acronym or initials—IBM started out as International Business Machines. There will be time, once your business becomes as well known as IBM, to introduce your acronym or initials. Avoid names that are too cute—you are a professional, so devise a corporate name and any tag lines that have the same tenor as those for a law firm or consulting company. By focusing on a particular type of business for a particular vertical market, you allow yourself the luxury of selecting a company name that is descriptive and memorable. A name such as Fiscal Statistics, Inc., gives a prospect a general idea about the work performed by your company—a banker who may need economic data in the future should be able to remember it. Jones Information Services is so generic it is meaningless. Information brokers have used the words information, facts, search, resource, and research in an amazing variety of combinations, abbreviations, and acronyms. The result is that many company names contribute nothing to establishing an identity for the company.

Before settling on a name, conduct a trademark search to determine if your name is being used by another firm and to reserve this name for your use. Look in:

- telephone directories: search the White and Yellow Pages
- county recording office: search the county clerk's Fictitious Business Name files
- information-broker directories such as the *Burwell Directory of Information Brokers* (www.burwellinc.com) and the *Association of Independent Information Professionals Membership Directory* (www.aiip.org/), or check with your local public library
- state corporate office: find out if a corporation is using your proposed name, even if you do not intend to incorporate at this time
- federal and state registered trademark databases: the federal trademark database is available on CD-ROM at some public libraries, and federal and state trademark databases are also accessible through Dialog and LEXIS-NEXIS.

If your chosen company name is not being used by another business, then file for its use following the procedures in your given state. In most states, you file a fictitious business name statement with the local county clerk/recorder and/or prepare and run a legal notice in your local newspaper that carries legal name announcements.

If your business will be incorporated, file a corporate name reservation with your state's office of the secretary of state or the department of corporation. This will provide statewide protection and use of your name as a corporation. It will not provide exclusive rights to your name outside of a single state unless you also register in other states. The simplest way to reserve a name is to register your name under state or federal trademark laws. If you are a corporation, the name of your business in most states must contain the words "Inc." or "Incorporated." Consider this when naming your company.

The name of your corporation and your business name do not have to be the same. If your business has a separate name from the corporation, your DBA, which stands for "doing business as," name can differ. This allows corporations to hold or own businesses with more than one name if they wish.

ESTABLISHING YOUR BUSINESS CREDENTIALS

Even if your firm will be a sole proprietorship with no employees, you must file appropriate forms with the IRS. If it is likely that the business will utilize contract employees, then it must also file information at tax time for these employees.

Use Federal Form SS-4 to obtain your business's federal employer identification number (FEIN), which is used for income tax reporting. There is no fee for obtaining this number. Once the IRS receives your application it will process your request and send you a nine-digit, identification number. You will have to have this number to open a bank account, establish an S-Corporation, file an income tax return, or make a tax deposit. If your business is established as a sole proprietorship, it may be also be possible to submit your taxes using your social security number rather than a FEIN.

Apply for a state employer number. Your state may require a state tax-identification number for your business if your business employs one or more persons and plans to pay wages. Contact your state's taxing authority to obtain more information.

Contact the Internal Revenue Service to receive information about the use of the W-4 Form. If your business hires employees, each employee must complete, sign, and date a W-4.

The Immigration and Naturalization Services Form I-9 is devised to ensure that employers do not hire illegal aliens. The employer keeps it on file. The form can be obtained from INS by calling 1-800-755-0777.

If you utilize contract employees, then you must fill out, by January 31, a Miscellaneous 1099 for each person receiving more than $600 in compensation during the previous year.

Selling products and not just services may make your business liable to pay local and state sales taxes. In general, sales taxes are not levied on services, but tax laws are changing in this area, so check with your local jurisdiction. States typically collect sales taxes for both county and cities, so get in touch with your state tax office concerning obligations to collect and submit these taxes and how to obtain the proper forms and procedures.

Unemployment taxes also are typically collected by a state agency. Your business will be liable for the payment of these taxes if there are employees. Check with your state's employment division regarding forms and procedures.

Find out at the earliest opportunity whether a business license is necessary, since failure to obtain a business license may result in fines or penalties.

Depending upon your state laws, your state may require that you hold a special license to perform information services work. In some states, every information broker must have an investigator's license.

If you are classed as an independent contractor, you must pay a self-employment tax contribution from your income. The self-employment tax will be calculated on the net profit from your business, not on your gross wages.

ESTABLISHING A BUSINESS LOCATION

Locating your business is a major decision. For small businesses, the major choices are whether to set up a business office in a commercial location or to work from home. There are advantages and disadvantages to each approach. If you decide to rent commercial space for your business, use a commercial real estate broker to help you find space and to assist in negotiating the lease. It will be worth the time and effort. Be sure to have your attorney review the lease before you sign it.

Expect that it will be hard to lease less than 500 square feet of space for your business, since office spaces are usually larger than this. When looking for space, choose a building that is compatible with your needs and those of the business. Commercial space is classed according to the type of amenities offered, so be familiar with these classifications before you search for space. Buildings classed as "A" have high-quality finish out (decor and fixtures) with marble floors, food service courts, and other amenities. "B" class buildings have basic elevators, parking, and less expensive finish out. "C" buildings are one step lower in finish and details. Generally speaking, the best value is a "B" building. Details to watch for in choosing a building are:

- Is there adequate parking that is free to tenants?
- Does the building have good "drive up" appeal?
- Is the landscaping maintained and appropriate?
- Are building public spaces clean and attractive?
- Are building tenants appropriate neighbors for your business?
- Is there secure, well-lit, off-street parking?
- Is the building secure after hours?

Also be aware that commercial leases are negotiated agreements between landlord and lessee, so find out what type of lease is used and the obligations incurred by the lessee. It may be possible to negotiate better terms than those written in the lease contract. Commercial leases can be complex, so have your attorney review it with an eye toward whether your lease has conditions for setoff, expenses caps, indemnity, default, subordination, noncompetition, and personal guarantees.

ESTABLISHING A HOME-BASED OFFICE

Before deciding to base your business at home and to work out of your house, make two important phone calls. Call the local zoning office and check zoning regulations for your area about working from home. Next, check with your local telephone company to ensure you can get extra telephone lines installed, that optical fiber service is available (versus older copper pair wiring), and which services (such as call waiting, call forwarding, and messaging) are accessible from your location.

Once you have established that your home can serve as an office, take these basic precautions to safeguard your investment:

- Examine your electrical system to verify it has sufficient electrical wiring and outlets to power your office equipment. If there are frequent power surges or drops in power or voltage in your area or region, consider buying an uninterruptible power supply (UPS) and a line conditioner. Install or use grounded outlets and surge protectors as appropriate to protect expensive equipment.
- As you establish your office, ensure that important equipment is not located where it could be damaged by leaking water from bathrooms or drain pipes, and that it is away from pipes that might freeze and/or burst.

- Protect your business against fire. Install a smoke detector near your office location, and keep a fire extinguisher in the office. Arrange for a safety deposit box to store originals of legal, corporate, and other important business papers, or have a professionally installed safe located in a secure area of your home. Buy a safe that is fire rated to withstand a two-hour fire.
- Guard your office against theft. Install dead bolts on doors and windows to secure your entrances and structure. One simple security measure is to install window coverings so that office space and equipment cannot be viewed from the exterior of the building. Consider attaching computer equipment to desks with locking devices. Maintain an inventory of business equipment with models, serial numbers, and other information along with a photocopy. Keep one copy in your safety deposit or other safe location in case of a casualty loss.
- Examine your property for possible liability problems. If business visitors come to your home office, ensure that walkways and other areas of your residence and office are free of hazards or structural problems such as overhangs, loose pavement tiles, area rugs, and dim lighting. Remove ice and debris from all accessways promptly.

TAX EXEMPTIONS AND THE HOME OFFICE

If your business is located in your home, the Internal Revenue Service may be more likely to audit your return, since deductions for home offices are widely regarded as "red flags" to the IRS. Home office expenses can be legitimately deducted as expenses, however, if the office is used exclusively and regularly for trade or business activities and is *one* of the following:

- the principal place of business, *or*
- a place to meet with patients, clients, customers, *or*
- located in a separate, freestanding structure.

It is important that the home office be defined by some form of boundaries from the rest of the home to meet IRS requirements. It cannot be used for any personal purposes, and must not also serve other functions such as a den or television viewing area for the children. Keep beds, televisions, stereos, and exercise equipment out of the area defined as a home office. IRS rules do allow business files to be stored in a separate area such as a utility room that also is used for personal purposes.

These categories of home office expenses can be deducted:

- basic business expenses: e.g., supplies, stationery, advertising, car expenses, business equipment rent and depreciation, taxes, salaries, and the like
- direct home office expenses: e.g., repairing a broken window or electrical connections, special cleaning
- indirect home office expenses: e.g., utilities, real estate taxes, casualty losses, mortgage interest or rent
- depreciation on office furniture and equipment: methods of depreciation are complex and should be calculated by your accounting professional.

Deductions are calculated according to how much of the home is used for business purposes. For example, if your home office is located in a 200 square foot former bedroom of your 2,000 square foot residence, you can allocate 10 percent of your home indirect expenses to business expenses.

LEASED SPACE ALTERNATIVE

If for one or more reasons you cannot lease commercial space and you do not want to establish an office at home, consider leasing an executive suite in an office building. For instance, suppose you do not have a credit rating to lease permanent space, you do not have the capital to set up an office, or you do not want to sign a commercial lease for three years. In these cases, an executive suite is a good option. Executive suites offer turnkey services, a fully furnished office with a reception area, use of a shared meeting room to meet with clients, and, typically, services including a receptionist, telephone answering service, and telephone, fax, and photocopier. The drawback to executive suites is that they are expensive. You pay for each and every service you use, which increases your costs.

FURNISHING YOUR OFFICE

Most information brokers rarely see their clients in person, conducting business primarily by telephone. Consultants usually meet with a client at the client's place of business. Consequently, as you select fur-

FURNISHING THE INFORMATION BROKER'S OFFICE

desk	telephone lines (two minimum)
comfortable chair	ISDN line (optional)
book shelves	answering machine or service
typewriter	fax machine
photocopier	surge suppressors
computer and software	uninterruptible power supply (optional)
modem	
laser printer	line conditioner (optional)
color ink-jet printer (optional)	postage scale
scanner (optional)	three-hole punch or report binder
telephone	door with lock

nishings for your office, you need not be concerned with impressing visitors. Rather, focus on functionality and economy. If you have a home office, a door with inside and outside locks is an essential element; nothing can destroy a professional image faster than a crying child or a barking dog. And, since information broker work requires concentration, you must be able to limit distractions and interruptions.

Decide whether you are going to lease your office equipment or purchase it outright. Leasing makes sense if you are unsure how fast you will grow, or if business conditions are changing rapidly. Leasing also makes sense if it is crucial to preserve your capital and cash flow; with a start-up business, cash flow is important. If you lease, be sure to inquire about early buyout provisions in the event that you have the cash to purchase your equipment. Leasing often makes sense for a telephone system, if you require extensive features, and for a photocopier.

Make office equipment purchases carefully, since the efficiency of the equipment you choose can affect your productivity. Here are some questions to help you evaluate potential equipment purchases:

- Do I need this equipment?
- How fast is this equipment in terms of pages per minute or pages sent per minute?
- What features do I need on this equipment?
- How will the equipment "pay" for itself in terms of increased efficiency?

- Are there less expensive alternatives to this equipment?
- How reliable is the equipment and how long will it last?
- Would it be less expensive to lease the equipment than to purchase it?
- Do I need to invest in other services once I add this equipment?

INFORMATION TECHNOLOGY SUPPORT

Your most significant start-up investment will involve your primary business tool, the computer. Read computer periodicals, talk with knowledgeable friends and associates, and determine the features and functions you will need. Reliability should be a key consideration. In general, you should purchase the fastest computer with the largest hard disk you can afford. Your minimum basic configuration should have:

Pentium® processor
32 Mb memory
large hard disk (3 gigabytes)
1.44 Mb floppy drive
CD-ROM drive
SVGA monitor
fax modem
mouse
keyboard
backup capability (tape, zip drive, etc.)
latest release of Microsoft Windows®
Optional:
    sound board
    speakers
    PC camera - CU - See Me®

Select software you are already familiar with, if possible. As with hardware selection, analyze your needs, then read reviews. For instance, if you know that your reports for clients will contain numerous charts, tables, and graphs, select a word-processing package that will allow you to incorporate spreadsheet data easily. If you will be buying a package that is completely unfamiliar, find out about the help-desk policy of the publisher, the availability of third-party books on the package, and the availability of local training classes. Make sure the tools are in place to enable you to reach a reasonable level of competence quickly. Figure 3–2 lists some of the popular packages for the basic functions.

Figure 3–2 Important Software Packages for Start-Up Businesses	
Accounting:	Quicken, QuickBooks, Expensible
Accounting and payroll (advanced):	Timeslips
Business and contact managers:	ACT, Microsoft Access
Word processing:	Microsoft Word, Corel, WordPerfect
Spreadsheets:	Microsoft Excel, Corel, QuattroPro
Presentations:	Microsoft PowerPoint, Harvard Graphics, Freelance Graphics, Astound, Director
Faxing:	WinFax
Internet browsers:	Netscape, Microsoft Internet Explorer
Other software:	Q & A, Norton Utilities, Uninstaller, Norton AntiVirus, McAfee Associates VirusScan

This list covers just the basics. Check with your local software dealer or review software in small business publications.

ESTABLISHING MAIL AND DELIVERY SERVICES

You need to arrange delivery services for your business. These may include U.S. Postal Service postage meter arrangements or a post office box for your business. A postage meter may be an important piece of business equipment if you do frequent mailings; be sure to include a postage scale and rate chart for determining charges.

Set up accounts with overnight and courier services. United Parcel Service and FedEx offer a variety of air and ground services and will come to your office location to pick up a package. You may also want to file a signature release form so you are not homebound whenever you are expecting a package. If you expect to have local delivery needs, arrange for a courier service in your area.

Repair services are critical to maintaining your office equipment. Determine reliable repair services (not service contracts, which we discuss below) from authorized repair outlets for:

- fax machine
- photocopy machine
- typewriter (yes, it still can come in handy for forms and labels)

Interview a computer repair person who can help you when disaster strikes. Prearrange this service and establish rates and availability before you need to call on it. Ask about the availability of pager numbers, response time, weekends, and overtime rates. Check out references for repair personnel and seek referrals from colleagues and friends.

Sales personnel for computers, copiers, and fax machines frequently push service contracts. Generally speaking, these contracts are expensive and not worth the fees. If the breakdown of a particular piece of equipment will devastate your business, however, then consider one. Similarly, if you are in a remote area, a service contract for a piece of equipment might make sense to avoid hourly costs for service personnel. Do not forgo this expense.

SOURCES

CITED IN TEXT

Brooks, Julie, and Barry Stevens. *How to Write a Successful Business Plan.* New York: Amacom, 1987, pp. 195–199.

FOR FURTHER INFORMATION

You can ferret out various sources of information on setting up your business. You might ask around your circle of family, friends, associates, and people already working for themselves. There are also trade associations, professionals such as accountants, lawyers, bankers, and other professionals you may meet through service groups such as the Chamber of Commerce, fraternal organizations, or merchant groups.

Government Sources

The U.S. Small Business Administration (SBA). There are local offices across the United States. Check the government section of your telephone directory for an office near you or call (800) 827–5722. The SBA publishes pamphlets on financial management, business planning and marketing. It also offers loans to small businesses (www.sbaonline.sba.gov).

Federal Information Center. This agency provides information on where to access government information and has local offices. Check the government listing of your telephone directory.

Economic development commission or offices. The city or county in your area may operate an economic development office that assists small, start-up businesses. Check with local and state government offices to determine if you are eligible.

Internal Revenue Service. Order two IRS publications: a tax pamphlet, *Tax Guide for Small Business*, publication 334 from the IRS; and *Business Use of Your Home*, publication 587, on the tax implications of operating a business from home. IRS, 1111 Constitution Ave North, Room 2315, Washington, DC, 20224. Order tax forms from (800) 829–3676.

Not-for-Profit Organizations

The Service Corps of Retired Executives (SCORE). Sponsored by the SBA, state and local governments, the educational community, and the private sector, SCORE has more than 13,000 retired executives nationwide who help individuals interested in starting their own businesses. SCORE provides free counseling, information, and training services. To locate a SCORE office in your area, check the telephone directory or call your local Chamber of Commerce or SBA office. The address for the national SCORE office is through the Small Business Administration, Suite 5900, 409 3rd Street, SW, Washington, DC, 20024.

National Small Business Development Center (SBDC). This organization provides location information on the 900 Small Business Development Centers in fifty states (www.smallbiz.suny.edu).

The Office of Women's Business Ownership. Another SBA division, this agency helps women in business. Phone: (202) 205–6673.

Minority Business Development Agency. A part of the U.S. Department of Commerce, this agency helps minority-owned businesses develop by providing management and technical assistance. Phone: (202) 482–5741.

National Association of Women Business Owners. There are forty-nine nationwide chapters of this organization, which addresses issues of concern to women entrepreneurs. Phone: (301) 608–3590.

Edward Lowe Foundation. This small biznet (www.lowe.org) contains a collection of 5,000 articles and documents on small business.

Colleges and Universities. Check with your local schools for programs about starting or running a business. Local community colleges are frequently good sources for courses on a variety of topics related to small business start-ups.

4 MANAGING YOUR PRACTICE

A small business owner needs support and advice from four important professionals: an accountant, a banker, an attorney, and an insurance agent. When selecting professional help, you will fare better if you avoid a large, national firm. Your business and you are likely to receive more time and attention and be able to negotiate a better hourly rate if you work with local professionals in small offices who enjoy a good local reputation. Ensure that your professionals know or work with clients in your type of business—which is a service business. If possible, look for advisors who work with small businesses, since they will expect you to ask questions and will be prepared to work with you on basic issues. For all your advisors, be sure to check references and verify credentials before signing on.

PROFESSIONAL SERVICES

In choosing your advisors, do three things. First, determine the type of advice you need (legal, general, etc.). Next, compile a list of potential advisors—ask friends and business associates, and check with local professional associations. Once potential candidates have been identified, screen and interview them.

Keep in mind that you should feel comfortable calling and talking with your advisors, otherwise you are less likely to go to them for advice when you need it. Questions to ask include:

- Do they provide the type of help you need?
- Do they have experience with similar-size clients?
- What will they do for you?
- What do they charge and how?
- Are they available to do your work?
- Do they understand your business needs?
- What are their cancellation conditions?

ATTORNEYS AND LEGAL ADVICE

Expect your lawyer to help set up your business structure and to provide legal advice. Your lawyer should be able to answer questions about contractual and tax matters and should review any lease or financial papers or agreements. Certainly consult your lawyer in any situation that might result in a lawsuit. The objective is to obtain good legal advice to avoid legal problems and lawsuits.

To find an attorney, start by getting information about lawyers in your area from the local bar association, which will be listed in your telephone directory. There may be a local lawyer referral service that can provide names. Consult a legal directory, which will give information on fields of practice and biographical information on lawyers. Also, consult colleagues, friends, and relatives who are in business.

ACCOUNTANTS AND ACCOUNTING SERVICES

Your accountant will advise you on tax and financial matters related to your business, particularly those related to federal and state tax requirements and issues. You do need to determine who will provide bookkeeping services—either yourself or a hired bookkeeper. A bookkeeper maintains your journal ledger and keeps track of assets and liabilities. This information is used to fill out various forms required by local, state, and federal jurisdictions. This information, once compiled, should be sent on to the accountant, who will prepare your tax return. Once your business develops a sizable staff, you might want to consider employing a payroll processing firm.

The most effective way to find a good accountant is to talk with others in your area who are in small service businesses. Your banker also may be able to make recommendations, as can friends, relatives, and colleagues.

BANKERS AND BANKING SERVICES

If you can, select a banker and not a bank. A banker can help you evaluate your business plan and may be critical to your success if you require start-up or ongoing financing for your business. Check with relatives and other business owners about their experiences with bankers and then interview a few. Friendliness and openness can be important characteristics in selecting one you can work with successfully. Select a bank that is large enough to offer commercial and personal banking services, but small enough to offer personal service. Compare the list of services offered by banks and check the schedule of fees for services. Most important, examine the loan policies and select a bank that is likely to make loans to small businesses.

INSURANCE AGENTS AND INSURANCE

Your best strategy in this area may be to select an insurance broker who works with an independent agency. Such agents represent several insurance companies and can write different types of insurance. They can obtain competitive bids from different insurance companies, ensuring a better price and better features for your insurance. If you are unfamiliar with the insurance company your policy is written on, go to the library and examine how well the firm is rated by Best—an independent rating agency that evaluates insurance companies based on their stability and performance.

If your business engages in consulting contracts with public agencies, clients may request evidence of your insurance coverage, or ask for information on it, such as the insurer's Best rating. Your company may also need to produce a certificate of insurance that states your policy coverage and limits. Ensure that your insurance company will be willing to provide this service, if required, when selecting the insurance firm.

If your personal insurance is already handled by an insurance agency, inquire about their capability to offer you additional types of insurance coverage for your business. Be sure that your insurance professional knows that you are in a service industry. Consider obtaining general liability and business automobile insurance. We will discuss specific insurance needs later in this chapter.

HIRING EMPLOYEES

One of the most important and difficult aspects of operating a business, especially a small business, is selecting, hiring, and managing employees. Small businesses are typically founded by entrepreneurially oriented individuals who may disdain management chores since their energy and attention are focused on making and marketing their services. There is often informal communication among employees. Employees tend to work long hours at modest salaries with the expectation that they will be provided with ownership benefits if the business is successful. So as your information-brokering business adds personnel, its organization will by necessity become more formalized. As you add staff, you may need to specialize job assignments more specifically, and to incorporate more sophisticated accounting systems. Management may need to create more formal communication methods to ensure that upper management provides direction, while lower level managers focus on operational and day-to-day management issues.

ALTERNATIVES TO EMPLOYEES

These days, there are several alternatives to adding full-time staff:

- *outsourcing or leasing*: The information-brokering firm enters into an agreement with a personnel leasing service that hires the broker's existing employees and then leases the employees' services back to the firm. The information broker gains the advantage that he or she no longer has employee administration costs for hiring, firing, or managing the personnel. The brokerage does not have to commit resources and time to functions that are secondary to its principal business purposes. The firm will pay from 15 to 36 percent of gross payroll for leasing costs.
- *temporary employees*: Consider hiring temporary employees for special tasks, but this alternative is more likely to be successful if you do not need a high level of staff skills and experience.
- *subcontracting*: A flexible arrangement is to subcontract with skilled professionals to perform specialized work or jobs of a specific duration. If your business loses a large client, you don't have to continue to bear the cost of a now-extraneous employee. Temporary workers and subcontractors are typically paid for work, however, before fees are collected from the client. This may be a disadvantage if your cash flow situation is lean.

Work suitable for subcontracting includes doing telephone research, cleaning up and formatting downloaded information, and document delivery. In certain cases it may be advantageous to subcontract for services you do not have the expertise to provide, such as patent searching or specialized searching in a scientific or technical area.

SUBCONTRACTORS OR EMPLOYEES?

The IRS's Form SS-8 helps determine whether a worker is an employee or an independent contractor. This form asks twenty questions about the status of the worker, such as whether the work is done under a written agreement, if the worker is given training by the firm, and so on. If your business does use contractors, be sure to file a Form 1099 (Miscellaneous Income) for each contractor who earns more than $600 a year through your company.

SUBCONTRACTOR CONTRACTS

If your business utilizes subcontractors, you should have a signed agreement with them that defines the following areas:

- the services to be obtained from the subcontractor, such as the hours and the rate to be paid for services

- the status of the subcontractor—that the subcontractor is not subject to employee withholding, unemployment contributions, insurance, and other employee benefits
- the ownership of materials and who owns the rights to materials
- a nondisclosure clause—a clause that states the subcontractor will not disclose sensitive client information
- who holds liability for any equipment or materials
- the conditions under which the agreement can be modified and other specifics.

Your attorney should be able to assist in the preparation of a subcontractor agreement form.

BASIC RECORD KEEPING

As a new business, it is important to establish a basic record-keeping system as soon as possible. Accurate records are essential for business planning and a big help when making management decisions about your business.

If you are a corporation, you can establish a fiscal year. It may have a different end-of-the-year date than a calendar year. Different fiscal year ends are an advantage for business with special needs, but in general an information-brokering business will have a calendar year as the fiscal year.

Internal Revenue Service requirements—as well as sound business practice—make it vital to maintain accounting records of your business's financial doings. In the case of an audit by the IRS, the auditor will expect to see documentation of all revenues and expenses reported on tax forms. While you are not obligated to share financial information on profits and losses with your clients, you will have to provide profit-and-loss statements to various agencies such as banks, credit card companies, and regional certification agencies if you are applying for MBE (Minority Business Owned Enterprise) or WBE (Women Business Owned Enterprise) status.

Basic record-keeping components include:

- business and corporate tax returns
- detailed operating statements
- financial statements
- information for tax returns and reports to regulatory agencies
- profit-and-loss statements
- sales-tax returns.

Deciding who should keep the books depends upon your abilities and time available to devote to this task. Software programs such as Quickbooks from Intuit Software or similar software programs make these tasks less onerous, although data must be entered regularly and accurately.

If you plan to have someone else keep your books, consider hiring a bookkeeping service to periodically compile receipts, list canceled checks, and process this information to compile financial statements.

RECORDS RETENTION

All businesses must store and retain records for a period of time. Currently the record retention requirements are as follows:

- Keep invoices, receipts, and costs records that support ledger entries for three years.
- Keep ledger entries indefinitely.
- Keep payroll and personnel records for four years.
- Retain contracts indefinitely.

Important records that should be kept include an expense ledger that lists cash and checks disbursed for expenses; employee compensation records listing hours, pay, and withheld deductions; and accounts-receivable records for credit sales.

INSURANCE

If your business has employees, and/or you are not covered by a spouse's policy, arranging for health and disability insurance is a must. Medical insurance coverage and rates are changing as medical and hospital services are restructured into HMOs (health maintenance organizations) and PPOs (preferred provider organizations). Check with your independent insurance agency for options in this area.

You must protect your business from casualty losses and liabilities. Basic insurance needs are: business property insurance to cover your business equipment, and furniture; automobile insurance to cover yourself and your vehicle for damage as well as coverage for damage caused by the driver of your car to other vehicles and people; liability insurance to protect against damages from others who may bring a suit against you. Your landlord may also require liability insurance if your business leases office space.

HOME OFFICE INSURANCE

Check your homeowner's policy carefully to determine if coverage includes the following:

- business property used in conducting a business
- minimum or maximum limits
- personal liability to persons arising from someone injured while visiting your premises for a business purpose.

Consider separate home-office insurance for your business. This type of coverage is just now becoming available in many states. Otherwise, try to acquire a home-office rider to your homeowner's policy or obtain separate business insurance coverage.

EMPLOYEE INSURANCE

If your business has employees other than yourself, consider additional insurance including workers' compensation, which protects employees from medical costs and lost income due to on-the-job injuries and protects your business from employee lawsuits over on-the-job injuries. Your state may require workers' compensation insurance. Even if it doesn't, if your business routinely works with state or local municipalities, universities, or state agencies, there may be contractual requirements that your business provide workers' compensation insurance if there is more than one employee.

Business interruption insurance may be useful and will protect against losses in case a fire or natural disaster closes down your office. Coverage can include from fixed expenses such as salaries, taxes and interest, and lost revenue in certain cases.

When you buy insurance, obtain rates from major, full-line insurance companies when possible. Compare bids, and look into taking a higher deductible for lower premium costs. First and foremost, however, find out if your existing personal insurance can be modified to cover your insurance needs before buying a separate policy; it could well save you money while giving you the coverage you need.

LIABILITY AND MALPRACTICE INSURANCE

Professional liability involves some form of misconduct by an information professional. Professionals, generally, are expected to be accountable and responsible for their behavior. There are a number of areas where liability can arise, including delivering incomplete or out-of-date data to a client, failing to consult the right source, or misrepresenting the work you are qualified to perform. Liability can occur from intentional carelessness or from simple ignorance. Whether librarians or information brokers can be sued for lapse of their professional responsibilities remains subject to debate, and so far there are few cases involving liability. Articles written about professional liability and professional malpractice consistently state that it is important that professionals exercise "reasonable care or prudence" in their work.

Lawsuits may arise over breach of contract, breach of warranty, and malpractice. Strictly defined, malpractice is professional negligence. *Harbeson v. Parke Davis* illustrates the problem of professional negligence; it found that malpractice resulted when medical personnel failed "to use information technologies . . . to gather data or to provide medical information from medical databases" (Froelich 1992). The risk of litigation can be mitigated by following these three basic rules:

- Establish operating procedures and follow them consistently.
- Be diligent about sources of possible omission negligence, such as accuracy and mistakes.
- Follow ethical guidelines for being an information professional.

There is errors-and-omissions insurance to cover professional liability. This type of insurance is expensive and often hard to find, and generally is intended to cover unintentional errors, not errors of judgment. Policies may differ according to whether they are "occurrence" policies, which cover claims made during the time the policy is in force, or "claims made" policies, which cover only claims made within the policy period.

DISCLAIMERS AND LIABILITY LIMITATIONS

To help stave off claims about services, use a disclaimer that alerts the client that you, as an information broker, are not offering a warranty on your services (Halvorson 1995). According to attorneys familiar with information-brokering work, disclaimers serve limited purposes and are not absolute protection. Information brokers also must be wary of describing services in brochures and collateral that make immodest claims or engage in "verbal puffery." Sample disclaimers follow.

SAMPLE DISCLAIMERS

1. The use of and reliance on any information provided by [Company Name] is at your own risk and discretion. [Company Name] makes no assurances as to the merchantability or fitness for a specific purpose of this information. [Company Name] shall not be responsible for any damages resulting from mistakes, omissions, errors, delays, or other defects in the information provided, or for any performance defect due to circumstances beyond the control of [Company Name]. The client hereby indemnifies [Company Name] against any claim for damages or loss [including copyrights and proprietary rights]. This indemnification shall not terminate with the termination of this service contract. [Company Name] will make every effort to locate the requested information and to check the accuracy of the information provided to the client, and will indicate all sources consulted. However, [Company Name] makes no warranty as to the accuracy or completeness of the printed information provided to the client. [Adapted from Rugge and Glossbrenner, 1992]

2. [Company Name] does not assume liability for the accuracy of data obtained from third parties, whether in machine-readable or printed form. [Company Name] makes no warranties or representations regarding the accuracy or completeness of information provided, and [Company Name] disclaims any liability for any damages in connection with use of its services.

SOURCES

CITED IN TEXT

Froelich, T. J. "Ethical Considerations of Information Professionals." *Annual Review of Information Science and Technology* 27 (1992): 302.

Halvorson, T. *Selected Aspects of Potential Legal Liabilities of Independent Information Professionals.* 2d ed., Houston, TX: Burwell Enterprises, 1995.

Rugge, Sue and Alfred Glossbrenner. *The Information Broker's Handbook.* New York: McGraw-Hill, 1992.

FOR FURTHER INFORMATION

Bureau of National Affairs is an independent publisher offering a Web site with information about their publications in the areas of human resources, environment, safety and tax management. (www.bna.com)

IRS help for small businesses is at (www.ins.ustreas.gov/prod/bus_info/index.html)

5 BILLING FOR SERVICES

This chapter looks at the all-important skills of pricing and selling your professional services to a prospective client. The second half of the chapter discusses how to develop and package your services in order to price and sell them attractively. In Chapter 7 we will discuss marketing your services as well.

HOW MUCH CAN YOU EARN AS AN INFORMATION BROKER?

A crucial element in your working with clients involves establishing an hourly or daily rate for your labor. The client will of course want to know, "How much will this cost?" The client sees "cost" as the price paid to the broker for the desired service, but the information broker must first calculate the cost of producing the product in terms of the daily labor rate for his or her services, plus overhead and the expected profit. The successful information broker will achieve a balance in setting fees that establishes a realistic fee schedule attractive to the client, but that also adequately compensates the information broker for the work performed. You must place a realistic value on your basic commodity—your time—and recover your ongoing overhead expenses.

How much to charge your clients will depend on these factors:

- your billing rate, which includes
  —your geographic location
  —how much you want to earn
  —your overhead expenses
- the nature of your services, which includes
  —the length of the project
  —the project expenses

Setting a labor rate is a three-step process. First, establish a reasonable salary expectation for yourself. Second, determine how many hours you must work to achieve your salary expectations and to pay your expenses. Third, make a reasoned estimate of your annual business expenses that must be covered in your billing.

STEP ONE: SETTING YOUR SALARY EXPECTATION
To establish a billing rate, first determine your salary expectation. Value your expertise and skills as an information broker as comparable to

those of a skilled research analyst or experienced reference librarian. Take into account what you feel you should be earning in your position with your experience. Your expectation and the position comparison method will give you a comfortable basis on which to set a daily labor rate. Using the determined salary level, then calculate a daily fee, exclusive of expenses, that estimates what you will work and be paid for.

For example, start with an annual salary expectation of $50,000. To determine the yearly labor rate, divide the expected annual salary of $50,000 by the number of days you will have to bill for work performed. This will result in a daily labor rate. Since there are 365 days in the year, and if you work eight hours each day, the rate to bill would be $136 per day. But since we do not work every day (holidays, vacation time), and because we have to engage in marketing and other duties that are not billable, we also have to calculate a reasonable estimate of the number of hours we are likely to bill each year.

STEP TWO: ESTABLISH THE AMOUNT OF BILLABLE TIME

Billable time is defined as the hours actually charged to a client. Experience indicates that once your business is established, expect to bill twenty hours of work per week. The rest of the time will go into the overhead of running the business, marketing, and personal time. Attorneys in large law firms can be expected to bill up to 7.5 hours per day, but they are responsible for producing work for clients, nothing else. As an information broker, it is more than likely your business will be a one-person affair, and that you will be responsible for all the tasks associated with keeping that business going as well as doing the work.

When first starting out, your billable hours may be a very small percentage of your week. Besides the fact that initially you may not have that many clients asking for your time, there are a number of activities that subtract from the potential number of billable hours available. Writing proposals, initial meetings with clients, preliminary research to facilitate estimating, calculating and presenting estimates, writing and paying invoices, collecting payments, planning, marketing, networking, training, and keeping up with events in your field, in business, and in your locale, all subtract from the time available for client projects. Initially, expect that planning, marketing, networking, and training will require a substantial commitment of your time.

The following examples of how to make a reasonable estimate of billable hours a year are based on Ann Wallingford's formula for rate setting (Wallingford 1996):

Subtract the following from 365 days:

Weekend days	104
Holidays	8–10 days
Vacation days	10–14 days
Sick days	5–8 days

Subtract days devoted to the overhead of operating the firm:

Administration, bill paying, bookkeeping, invoicing	24 days
Marketing, talking to prospective clients	34 days
Training	5 days

Depending upon the exact numbers you use, you can expect that you will have between 165 and 180 billable days per year. To arrive at a billable rate that will yield a salary of $50,000, divide $50,000 by 180 billable days (or if you only want to work 160 days, use that figure) to arrive at a daily labor rate of $277 per day, or an hourly rate of $35.

STEP THREE: CALCULATING OVERHEAD COSTS

After you have calculated the daily labor rate, account for how you will cover the cost of operating the business. These expenses are considered "overhead" and they differ from direct expenses that are incurred on behalf of a client while working on a job. Your estimate of yearly overhead fixed expenses include items such as office rent, office equipment and supplies, accounting, marketing, and advertising. Overhead expenses are difficult to calculate when just starting in business, but will become easier to estimate as time passes. Overhead expenses would typically include the following items:

- accounting and legal expenses
- automotive expenses
- business licenses, taxes
- business travel expenses
- clerical support
- dues and subscriptions
- equipment—computers, facsimile machine, photocopier
- employment taxes
- insurance
- marketing
- office rent

- personnel benefits—sick leave, retirement
- professional development, seminars
- stationery and supplies
- telephone.

Once you have determined your estimated overhead costs, divide this figure by the number of billable days and add this cost to your billable rate. For instance, if you determine that your annual business expenses are $10,000, then divide $10,000 by 165 days (or the number you used for your hourly rate), which results in a rate of $60.60 per day. This means you will need to add this amount to your billable rate to cover not only your salary but also your business expenses.

Many professional firms, rather than calculating a figure for actual expenses, use a multiplier to establish an overhead cost that is added to their cost proposals. Professional firms such as law firms and architects charge overhead fees as a common practice. Overhead percentages vary, but generally overhead rates are calculated at between 80 and 150 percent of the daily labor rate (Shenson 1990).

Finally, determine what you will charge as "profit," which is typically calculated at around 15 up to 40 percent of cost.

In the event that you are establishing a labor rate for an employee, multiply the annual salary by 1.5, which includes the approximate costs for insurance, health, and other benefits.

CONSIDERING THE GEOGRAPHIC MARKET

Now it's time to come to terms with the reality of the marketplace. Your hourly rate is going to depend to some extent on your costs, but also on what the market will bear. Since initially the majority of your clients will be in your geographic vicinity, call other information brokers in your area and find out their rates. Do not set your rate lower than everyone else. Be sure to get a good idea of what the going rate is for services similar to yours in your area. Rates for researchers on the West Coast, for instance, are twice those of researchers in the Midwest.

Now compare the rates your competitors charge with your calculated rate. If your rate is substantially higher, more than 30 percent, either lower your overhead costs or your salary expectations. Unless your business or your services offer some obvious advantages that your competitors lack, you risk pricing yourself out of the market. The justification for your higher rate must be absolutely clear to potential clients. If your rate is substantially lower than those of your competitors, potential clients may not take your services seriously. Are there potential overhead items that you neglected in your calculations?

Setting the correct rate is essential because once you have an established clientele, it will be difficult to raise your rates. Your clients will have become used to receiving a certain amount of service per dollar, and by raising your rates you may run the risk of losing clients.

HOW TO PRICE YOUR SERVICES

The second set of factors that will influence your income as an information broker involves how your services are priced and billed. Most information brokers who provide research services charge an hourly rate plus out-of-pocket expenses, which may include database usage fees, long-distance telephone costs, copyright charges, photocopy charges, travel-related expenses such as mileage and parking, and courier charges. Depending on the sources used and the type of request, the added out-of-pocket expenses may be as much as 80 percent of the total amount charged to the client. For instance, retrieving a mailing list from an online database takes very little time but can be enormously expensive in terms of database charges. The more value added to a research project in terms of analysis, the higher the proportion of project fees you keep.

Information brokers perform research work for clients with more money than time. Keep in mind that informaton brokerage services involve charging for a service, not selling information. Be sure your client understands that you expect to be paid for your research efforts even if the specific information desired is not available.

There are two common methods of billing for services. If you understand your service and can reasonably estimate the cost to produce it, then setting up a fixed-price contract with the client that estimates a set amount of labor and overhead expenses is the best practice. As we discuss later on in this chapter, as your business grows, you will become more skilled at estimating price packages for certain services. The fixed-price method is preferable if you and your client have a good understanding of the work expected to be performed. A survey of consulting professionals found that those offering fixed-price contracts exceeded the estimates of costs 24 percent of the time, with poor estimating skills the reason given for failure in most cases (Shenson 1994).

An alternative is to offer a service on a pay-as-you go method, whereby a project is executed according to a daily or hourly rate and you bill as you do the work. This type of service contract is best when the assignment is difficult to estimate or if the work statement is not well-defined. A form of a pay-as-you-go contract is a time-plus-materials contract, in which you track time spent on the project and out-of-pocket costs and submit a time sheet and receipts along with an invoice at specified intervals. Time-plus-materials contracts protect the information broker from "piling on" by the client, where the client adds to the scope of the work in incremental steps until a project has grown significantly. With a time-plus-materials contract, changes to the scope of the project may mean working more hours, but you can also expect to be paid for them.

ESTIMATING

Unless the client is merely price shopping, your hourly rate will not be nearly as significant to the client as the total cost of the project. When potential clients call, their first question is usually, "Can you find this information?" The second is, "How much will it cost?" It may be possible to give a ballpark estimate based on similar searches you have done in the past. Estimating requires knowing something about what a "typical" search might involve, but some searches are more easily defined than others. For instance, a profile of a private company might cost between $100 and $200; a software search would generally fall in the same range. Newspaper searches for articles about a particular person, company, or event are absolutely impossible to estimate because there is no way to know the extent of coverage beforehand. The cost depends entirely on how many times the name or subject appears in the database. You're as likely to win the lottery as to give a correct estimate on a newspaper search.

Whether or not the client asks for an estimate, you should establish a budget for the project. If costs are not directly addressed, you and the client may have dramatically different figures in mind—an unfortunate situation if your figure is the higher one. But an estimate may be quite difficult to give unless you have performed similar projects in the past, so, if possible, have the client set a "not to exceed" limit. If the budget begins to look inadequate as the project proceeds, call the client and renegotiate the limit. If this doesn't work, you have two options. One is to limit the scope of the research, making sure that the client understands what portion of his or her original request has been eliminated; consider writing up a "scope of research" statement and fax it to the client. The danger with limiting the search is that the client will remember the initial request, not the modified version, and will not be satisfied with the results. The second option is to refer the client to other sources such as the public library or the Internet.

Yet another strategy is to invite the client to set a budgetary limit. This is effective when the client is not very communicative. For instance, a corporate profile may mean one thing to you and another to your client. The same is true for a market profile. If you cannot find out what information the client expects to receive, find out the spending cap. A client who has $200 to spend on a market profile is going to get much less information than one who has $1,000. Give the client an idea of what to expect for a specific amount of money.

A good guideline is to tell the client to be prepared to spend $50 on even the simplest request. In certain circumstances it may be better to turn down a project than accept too small a budget. If you accept a project in which you lose money, you could wind up resenting the client, and it is not worth the stress of having to watch the clock and thus not being able to do a quality job because the project does not have enough money. If you cannot get the client to set a budgetary limit, offer a range. Do not be afraid to quote high; at that point, the client will usually set a limit.

STRATEGIES FOR PRICING SERVICES

To create a more stable cash flow, attract new business, or increase business from your existing clients, explore alternative methods of pricing services. The most commonly used methods are memberships or retainers and pricing strategies such as flat-fee or unit pricing. Each of these types of pricing strategies are not exclusive, and the information broker may wish to suggest one or more pricing strategies to a client depending upon client needs and understanding of the client's project and budget.

Retainers

In this type of service, commonly offered by attorneys or lobbyists, you can sell a preset amount of services each month to a client. The advantage of this pricing method is that it guarantees the client a certain amount of work each month at a preset, or not-to-exceed, billing amount. The retainer offers the information broker a predictable income stream, which gives the broker the leeway to offer the client a discounted price for these services.

Deposit Accounts

Some information brokers encourage their clients to set up deposit accounts in which the client pays the information broker a substantial sum and the broker deducts payment from the account as work is performed. The client does not have to deal with multiple invoices, and the information broker does not have to wait for payment. Requiring a retainer for relatively small projects may actually discourage clients from using your services, especially if they need a quick turnaround. Some projects require same-day turnaround, which does not allow time to mail a retainer fee.

Memberships

An information broker can offer an annual membership to clients, who pay a fee (in addition to fees for services) up front before any work is performed. This strategy eliminates those potential clients who are not serious prospects and encourages an ongoing relationship with those who are. The disadvantage is that it eliminates many of the "one-shot" clients who, while not a source of continuing business, are a source of immediate income. One possibility is to offer memberships with discounted hourly rates, while still accepting clients at a full rate who are not willing to make the membership commitment. A membership package includes the special discount rate on searching services, priority turnaround for requests, a free newsletter, or other special benefits.

Package Pricing

Certain types of research projects in which the results are relatively predictable and the scope controllable lend themselves to package pricing. For instance, the FYI service from the County of Los Angeles Public Library provides a basic trademark search for a fixed price of $125 (www.colapublib.org/fyi) that produces a package containing brief information on interpreting the results of the search along with lists of conflicting trademarks. When FYI locates numerous potential conflicts, the output is limited to those that are particularly relevant.

In order to provide a fixed price for research, the results must be controllable. Searches of newspapers for articles on a company, for example, cannot be effectively packaged, since the results may be no articles or dozens, even within a restricted time period. If there are limitations placed on the output, they must be easily explained and logical; they cannot be arbitrary or appear to the client to be arbitrary. The price charged for a packaged product must be high enough to cover costs and yield a profit for nearly all searches of that type, but not so high as to discourage potential customers. Assuming that the client understands the costs associated with producing certain information products and services, it is possible to offer these services based on a flat-fee cost.

The simplest form of package pricing is to offer a one-day consulting engagement to the client. Other examples of package pricing include performing a subject-based database search of a specific set of databases for a client. Another popular package is to sell a "current awareness update" service to a client on a topic of continuing interest.

Unit pricing

Certain services can be priced by the item or unit, but arriving at effective unit pricing may be difficult. It works well if you are offering cataloging services or other services when it is not clear as to the number of units or the magnitude of the work. The advantage for the client is the ability to pay for work as it is performed, thus spreading costs over time. For instance, you can bill on an ongoing basis for the number of books cataloged.

ADJUSTING FEES

In general, it is a bad practice to lower your daily labor rate for services if you feel that a competitor is about to underbid you or because of pressure from a client. If your work proposal is calculated correctly with the right amount of labor, then do not engage in the practice of discounting your daily labor rate.

Occasionally, a client who has received a proposal may ask to negotiate the cost. A good technique to use in this situation is to break the proposal into sections and assign a cost to each section. To reduce the overall cost of a project, the client must then eliminate certain tasks. This method allows you to maintain your base rate, cover your overhead, and make a profit on those hours you apply to the project. It is not a good practice, however, to reduce your estimate without reducing the scope of the project. Your credibility with the client may be damaged, and you will have difficulty maintaining your base rate. If the client refuses to accept the quoted price and refuses to reduce the scope of the project, you may have failed to explain adequately what is involved and the potential benefits, or the client may have had unreasonable expectations from the outset. Most consultants write several proposals for every one that is accepted.

In certain circumstances, it may be advantageous to offer a client a price that is a sale or discounted price—that does not fully cover overhead costs—due to an expectation of future business with that client. Continuing to price services at levels that do not account for overhead and labor costs, however, means that the business will operate at a loss and not survive.

A FINAL WORD ABOUT PRICING

Do not expect to make a profit your first year, but do try to cover your expenses. Make sure your bank balance is large enough so you can avoid cash-flow problems. Keep a close eye on the bank balance and plan for bills that will come in. If you perform an online searching service, it is likely the invoice from the online service will be due and payable before your client pays for the search.

Do not expect to make a fortune, ever. Do not underestimate how much of your time will be taken up by things that are not billable. Marketing, talking to prospects, preparing proposals, paying bills, making collection calls, and sending out statements all require time. In addition, just about everything information brokers do is intellectually demanding. Every now and then you will want to take a break just to give your brain a rest.

SOURCES

CITED IN TEXT

Shenson, Howard, *The Contract and Fee-Setting Guide for Consultants and Professionals*. New York: John Wiley, 1990, p. 6.
———. *Shenson on Consulting*. New York: John Wiley, 1994.
Wallingford, Ann. "Guide for Rate Setting." Freelance Online Open Forum [FAQ], October 8, 1996, at 10:50 a.m. Available: www.freelanceonline.com/messages/426.html

PART III
FINDING AND SERVING YOUR CLIENTS

WORKING WITH CLIENTS

This chapter discusses two of the most difficult aspects to being an information broker: working with clients and getting them to pay. These problems really stem from the fact that information is intangible. You cannot show it to a prospect nor guarantee results. A related issue is that while information has a definite cost, its value is relative—like beauty, it is in the eye of the beholder.

INTERVIEWING AND NEGOTIATING WITH CLIENTS

Negotiating how to frame and how to answer a question for a client are two of the most important processes and skills that an information broker can possess. There are two skills related to this question-and-answer negotiation process: interviewing, and effective negotiation. When a prospect calls, you first must find out not only exactly what the client needs but what value the client puts on that information. It is also important to determine if the client is willing to pay for a search that may not result in the information needed. All the while you're trying to find out about the client, you must also be conveying confidence, competence, and professionalism.

This interview process is really what librarians call the "reference interview." In an ideal world, a client would identify a problem, determine what information would assist in developing solutions, and request that the information broker locate that information. The real world is different. According to Jeffrey Katzer, professor of library science at Syracuse University, "Today's user is more likely to find a problem, take action to solve it, and then collect the information to support his action" (Feldman 1996). Clients who have not experienced the overwhelming amount of information on the Internet tend to ask for "everything" on a subject on the assumption that there is not much available. Other clients try to make your life easier by asking for what they think your business can provide without knowing if it will actually contain what they need. In many instances, the client has not thought through the problem enough to identify what information is needed. A client might say he needs an annual report on a company, when what he really wants is a breakdown on market share for the company and its competitors. An ad agency account manager may be certain the campaign her client is suggesting is not a good idea, but may not know how to convince the client he or she is wrong.

As the world of information becomes more crowded and complex, as sources proliferate and pricing schemes become more labyrinthine, the valuable services provided by the information broker move from just locating information to diagnosing the need and identifying the best source. For the experienced researcher or consultant, providing the information is the easy part. Working with the client to analyze the problem correctly and identify potential solutions (or justifications for the solution already implemented) requires considerable skill.

COMMUNICATING WITH CLIENTS

In the best of circumstances, the information broker and the client communicate well because they both understand the question and the information that is required to proceed with the research. Other factors, however, can complicate the question negotiation process, most typically:

- Clients will ask for what they think you can supply. Therefore, you need to develop the most tactful ways of interrogating clients to find out their exact needs. For example, you can say, "Is there something particular in the annual report you need? It's much less expensive if we retrieve just part of the report rather than the whole thing."
- Clients often do not know what they want or what they need, even though they think they do. An illustration of this is the "I need information on Company X" request. When you ask the client to specify the kind of information, the answer may well be, "Whatever you can find." If Company X is public, responding to this parameter can bury the client in information and cost the client a small fortune. If the company is private, your searching can be expensive and result in only little bits of information that may not help the client at all. You must take the time to explain that certain information on private companies is not going to be available, or your client will be disappointed regardless of how good a job you do.
- Client can be secretive. Ask how the client is going to use the information. This question often leads to a very wide-open discussion that brings up information needs the client may not have thought about and gives an insight into unstated format requirements. Unfortunately, some clients refuse to say why they need the information. All information brokers must promise and maintain client confidentiality, yet even long-time clients will some-

times be unwilling to discuss the background of a research project, believing that the problem is articulated sufficiently and you do not need to know any more. For example, a client once asked for market research on athletic shoes. Her company was not in the shoe business, but the marketing manager refused to give more information. The client would have received a much better search of articles if the information broker had known why the client's company needed the information. Were they going to manufacture shoes, were they considering a joint marketing arrangement with a shoe manufacturer, or did they want to license their name to a shoe manufacturer?

The "Johari Window," a concept borrowed from psychology, can be used to help determine the efficiency of communication. It demonstrates in a simple way how client and broker may find themselves in different states of knowledge and awareness when negotiating the level, type, and amount of information to be defined and then gathered (see Figure 6–1).

Figure 6–1 Johari Window

	Known to broker	Not known to broker
Known to client	Perfect	Guarded
Not known to client	Seeker	High Risk

Each window represents the state of knowledge of the client and the broker. On the left, you possess equivalent or more information than the client and therefore must help to define the client's requirements before proceeding further. In the "perfect" condition, you and the client are both confident that you understand what is requested and needed. In the "seeker" situation, however, you may be in more of a position to influence the size and extent of the search because of the lack of knowledge on the part of the client. It is your responsibility to exercise appropriate judgment in selecting the type of sources and the extent and limitations of the search. You have an obligation to keep the client informed.

On the right-hand side, the client may possess more information than you do. Expect that in many cases the client will have more subject expertise than you. In some instances, the client does not choose to reveal all of the information about his or her needs. In the "guarded" situation, the information broker learns enough about the subject from the client to evaluate intelligently the information retrieved. Do not be afraid to admit knowing nothing about the moisture content of concrete; the client probably knows little about searching engineering databases. Even without specialized knowledge, you should be able to provide the client with guidance on the type of information that will likely be available, the difficulty of obtaining that information, search strategies to be used, and some indication of the costs involved. The client, on the other hand, may be able to suggest sources of information such as periodicals or trade associations. Expect the client to assist in defining industry-specific terminology—whether you search online databases or call experts, knowing the terms conventionally used for a topic is essential.

In the final case, in which both you and the client may be unfamiliar with the subject or area, you must first apprise the client of this and then endeavor to keep the client's lack of knowledge from limiting or affecting the search results. In this circumstance, you may have to do more work to ensure that you have provided accurate and sufficient services to the client.

In diagnosing a research need, the most effective question is, "How will you use the information?" The answer should not only reveal what information is needed but also give you an outline of format requirements and time frame. Open-ended questions allow the client to "think aloud." Try to suggest types of information other clients have requested to solve similar problems—without, of course, breaching the confidentiality of the other clients. The more precisely you can identify the client's need, the more likely you are to satisfy it. A client with only a vague idea of what he needs means you run the risk that, when you deliver your product, the client may decide that the product is not what was wanted. Avoid, if possible, getting into the situation in which clients say they will know the information when they see it, and this is not it. If a client asks for "market research" on an industry, ask what the client expects to receive. If the client wants "background on a company," use the checklist in Figure 6–2 to determine exactly what elements should be included. Incorporate the checklist in those situations where the client is too inarticulate to respond to open-ended questions; in most cases, clients are not trying to be obtuse; they simply have not given enough consideration to the prob-

Figure 6–2 Company Information Request Checklist

Do you need financial information?

    For just the current year?

    Just earnings or a balance sheet?

    Do you need performance ratios?

    Do you need information on assets or how fast the company pays its bills?

    Do you want information on stock price fluctuations?

Do you need information on subsidiaries?

    Just a list or addresses and officers?

Do you want just a corporate profile?

Do you need information on executives?

    Just a list or biographical details?

    Do you need to know about his/her relationships with other companies?

    Do you need articles on the executive?

    Do you need articles or speeches by the executive?

Do you need product information?

    Descriptions of individual products, or just a line of business overview?

    Do you want product reviews or just product introduction announcements?

Do you need information on advertising and marketing strategy?

    Do you want details on ad campaigns?

    Do you need market share information?

    Do you want articles on past marketing strategy?

    Do you want articles on future plans?

    Do you want a market forecast?

Do you need competitor information?

    Do you want just a list of competitors or background on each?

Do you want background on the industry as a whole?

lem to know what they need. For those who are not aware of your resources, ignorance of the possibilities may make specifying the need difficult.

A consulting project involves a similar but somewhat more complicated approach. It may be relatively straightforward to identify the problem, such as providing basic end-user searching capabilities to a range of departments. But you need intuition and interpretive skills to determine which of the available solutions will be acceptable to the client. Questions of territory and control may make the obvious and most logical solution unacceptable. Calling in a consultant may be the result of a hidden agenda. As with the research interview, listen carefully, pursue the implications of seemingly casual comments, and make sure you understand the environment as well as the specific problem.

CLIENT PROPOSALS

Once you understand the requirements of the assignment, you can develop a proposal. For assignments that will be billed at less than $500, a verbal wrap-up should be sufficient. Proposal development takes time, so writing a proposal for relatively small research assignments is not cost effective. A clear verbal summation, however, is necessary. If your interview with the client has been lengthy and if you have "worked through" the problem during the conversation, be sure that you and the client reached the same end point—your analysis of the project may be very different from the client's initial request. Conclude your conversation with a brief statement of the exact information to be provided, the expected or not-to-exceed cost, and the delivery date. For example, "We will obtain the ABC Company's most recent annual and quarterly reports, daily stock prices for the last thirty days, and articles from the last month in newspapers and business magazines on the CEO's indictment; the cost is not to exceed $500, and we will deliver the results by the close of business on Wednesday."

For larger research projects and for consulting projects, you may need to prepare a more formal proposal, which should include the following elements:

1. *A statement of the problem to be solved.* For instance, gain an understanding of the company's position in relation to its fifteen major competitors, or provide desktop access throughout the company to the library's resources.
2. *A statement of methodology.* For a research project, this section would outline types of information to be obtained and/or sources.

For instance, in the research case above, sources would include annual reports of competitors, analyst reports on competitors and the industry as a whole, articles in trade magazines that evaluate the company's products and those of its competitors, and the like. The methodology for setting up access to library resources may involve integrating the library's OPAC with the corporate intranet. In writing this section of the proposal, manage the level of specificity carefully. If the methodology is too clearly spelled out, an unscrupulous client may use the proposal as a guideline for performing the project in-house or for writing a contract with another vendor. Too much specificity may also limit you, since you may discover better sources or better methods for accomplishing the project goals as you go along. Try not to have the proposal restrict your ability to utilize what you learn as the project progresses. At the same time, however, provide enough specificity to convince the client that you have the capability to accomplish the project.

3. *A list of deliverables.* This section describes exactly what the client will receive. It may be a report summarizing the competitive position of fifteen companies with complete text of all sources used; an analysis of several OPAC software packages and a recommendation of one; procedures for uploading catalog data to an intranet; or selection and installation of OPAC software, conversion of catalog data, uploading of data to an intranet, and procedures for maintaining the system. This section should be very specific. Often final payment is contingent on "acceptance" of the product as described in the proposal. Careful definition of the deliverables also prevents expansion of the project by the client without a comparable increase in the fee. If a client is not satisfied at the end of a project, you should at least be able to show that you have delivered what was specified in the proposal. If the proposal is lengthy or complex, ask a friend or associate to read it. Be sure there is no room for misinterpretation of the promised results of the project.

4. *Cost and payment requirements.* Estimating is always difficult. In general, overestimating by a small amount is preferable to underestimating. If the final cost of a research project is somewhat less than the estimate, the client will be pleased. Serious overestimating, however, may prevent your receiving the assignment. If you are unsure what to charge, call a more experienced information broker, explain the project, and ask if your estimate seems reasonable. When setting a fixed price for a consulting project, consider doubling your initial estimate of the hours that will be required. Give careful consideration to the time that will not be under your control, such as meetings with the client, the

MIS department, or vendors. For large projects, you will probably want partial payment at identifiable milestones. This helps your cash flow and also prevents a substantial sum from being withheld if a dispute arises over the deliverables at the end of the contract. Although such disputes should be rare, the occasional, unreasonable client is probably inevitable.

COLLECTING PAYMENT

The most important factor in collecting payment for your services is the satisfaction level of your clients. To maintain a high satisfaction level, you must manage your clients' expectations. Give an adequate diagnosis of the problem, a clear statement of the scope of the project and project deliverables, and comprehensible explanations for any deviation from the promised results. Clients who are not satisfied are more likely to refuse to pay or to delay payment than those who are. There are several common reasons for collection problems, and most are avoidable.

- *Failure to follow client company accounting procedures.* If your client is a major corporation, be sure that your contact person is authorized to spend money. Ask if a purchase order is required, and include the purchase order number on your invoice. Send your invoice to your contact person for approval; sending the invoice to accounts payable causes delays as it is passed about the company collecting necessary signatures.
- *Failure to invoice in a timely manner.* Your invoice should accompany your report to the client, especially for a relatively small project. If you wait two to three weeks, the client may have forgotten what you provided and your invoice may get lost in a sea of more critical items.
- *Client cash flow problems.* If your clients are small businesses, try to avoid being caught in the domino effect of delayed payment. If the client waits to receive payment from a third party before paying you, your payment may be delayed for sixty to ninety days. Keep close tabs on the outstanding balances of small company clients. If a balance becomes large or if payment has not been made in a month, notify the client that no further assignments can be accepted until payment has been received. Although cutting off a client is difficult, if the client does not pay, you are better off not accepting the work.

A credit-card merchant account is an excellent way to solve payment problems for small clients. Depending on the state in which your business is located, however, it may be difficult to obtain. If you cannot get one, ask a prospective client to fax you a brief statement of their research request, their budget, and an acknowledgment that your invoice will be paid within a specified time. For larger projects, request that the client sign an acknowledgment line on the proposal and fax it back.

How do you protect yourself from clients failing to pay? Keep up with the accounts receivable. Know who owes money. Do not let their outstanding balances get too large. Do not be afraid to tell a client you would like to have some sort of payment on the account before you do another job. When accounts are more than thirty days old, start calling your clients to find out when you can expect payment. On the first call, ask if they need another copy of the invoice; in some cases that is all they need—things do get lost in both the U.S .and interoffice mail. On the second call, ask when you can expect a check. Pursue a client for seventy-five days. After that your chances of collecting are slim, and the debt can be written off. Also, keep track of who the deadbeats are for, amazingly, they will call again. Tell them you will be happy to do another project if they pay their outstanding balance and half the estimate for the proposed project.

Effective communication is the key ingredient for satisfactory relationships with clients. By understanding the client's needs, you will be able to produce a high quality product. By meeting the client's needs, you will ensure payment of your fees and be likely to have repeat business from that client.

SOME PRACTICE SCENARIOS

Here are some sample scenarios that might help you to estimate the time and effort required to produce an "answer" for the client. Remember to include time to format the results.

A client is starting a new business in the area of corporate and records management and wishes to automate the business. The client wants to know what software packages are available—the types of packages, their prices, their capabilities, and how each package compares with one with which he is familiar.

A client is starting a travel business and needs to find mailing-list brokers to market a niche business. The client is interested in obtaining information about national and regional lists and wants specifically to target female professionals who are interested in arts and crafts and archaeology and have a household income of more than $50,000 per year.

A client is interested in starting a new business designing and selling fitness equipment, specifically a stair-climbing exercise machine. She wants to know the primary advertising outlets for fitness machines, who manufactures these machines, what manufacturing methods and materials are used, the total annual sales for the most recent year, how the products are distributed, and what share of the market each product has.

A publisher would like to start a regional or a city magazine as a new business. He would like to know how many of these types of products exist, what markets they cover, their annual sales, and projected growth.

A pharmaceutical industry consultant needs information about hair restoration products for the treatment of male pattern baldness. She wants to know the results of medical studies published in the last six months, an update on any studies under way, the name of the most effective remedy on the market, and the annual sales for this product.

A client wants advance notice of all area code changes in the United States. He wants to know if there is a mailing list to subscribe to. He wants to receive notification of the area code changes and the specific exchanges or parameters that will be changing.

Your firm has been contacted by a new "trade mart" that sells retail selling space to clients in the communications/telecommunications/computing and electronics and related industries. They would like a proposal regarding how to go about setting up a library of about 20,000 volumes with two staff members. They also want to know what services the library should offer.

A client wants to know how many U.S. hospitals have libraries with two or more full-time (FTE) staff. Can the hospitals be identified somehow—such as hospitals with over 200 beds that have staffed libraries?

A client would like to market services to small grocery stores—"mom and pop" type of businesses. She wants to characterize these types of businesses and wants to know how much information is obtainable on each store in order to establish a direct-marketing campaign.

A client wants to know how many manufacturing companies are within a 300-mile radius of Louisville, Kentucky, that manufacture automotive parts and services and appliances (or the SIC [Standard Industry Code] code of 3631).

A client wants to establish a business manufacturing ergonomic office chairs that compete on quality, not price. The client would like to know who is in this market, how the prices run, and the distribution channels. This client also wants to retain the services of an ergonomics expert and wants to know qualifications and availability.

SOURCES

CITED IN TEXT

Feldman, Susan. "The Online World 1996 Conference," *Information Today* (December 1996): 14.

FOR FURTHER INFORMATION

Another application of the Johari Window to information brokering appears in an article by Donna Shaver and Nancy Hewison, "Ethics for Online Intermediaries," *Special Libraries* (Fall 1985): 238–245.

7 MARKETING YOUR BUSINESS

We have already discussed the need for a business plan. A major component of that plan is an examination of the market for your services. The marketing plan expands on that analysis by outlining how your services will be presented and promoted to potential clients. A marketing plan should be developed for each individual product or service you plan to offer. Like the business plan, the marketing plan should be an outline that changes as the business adapts to altered client and market conditions.

The critical elements of the marketing plan are:

- Product/Service definition
  —Exactly what does your company produce and sell?
- Production ingredients
  —What are the raw materials and work skills that are required to produce the product or service?
- Target market
  —Whom do you expect to buy the product or service?
  —How is this group characterized?
- Competition
  —What other sources can your target market use to obtain the same product or service?
- Sales/Revenue goals
  —How much of the product or service will you sell?
  —What will be your profit?
- Promotional plan
  —How will you convince those in the target market to purchase the product or service from you?

All of these elements are closely interrelated. As the marketing plan develops, you will probably redefine and revise some of them several times. Designing a product or service that is desired by a sufficiently large number of customers and is priced to provide an adequate profit without discouraging sales requires talent and often inspiration.

DEFINING THE PRODUCT/SERVICE

Begin with a description of the product or service's physical characteristics. If the service is on-demand research, the product may be a report comprised of the text of articles, summaries of telephone interviews, a list of companies and contacts, and an analysis that relates these materials to the problem the client is trying to solve.

Now describe the product or service from the client's point of view. How will the client use it? What are the benefits to the client? This step is particularly important, since this information will be used in analyzing the market and the competition and in developing promotional materials. Research services might benefit clients by giving them confidence in the correctness of decisions, allowing them to take advantage of changing market conditions, or saving them time.

In your description of the product be as specific as possible—from both your viewpoint and that of the client. Consider subdividing a major category such as "consulting" into several specialties: floor-plan design, selection of software for library catalogs, sensitivity training for public service staff. Select those areas you enjoy the most.

PRODUCTION INGREDIENTS

The next step is to identify what you need to produce the product or service. These items fall into two categories: raw materials and work skills. For a research service, raw materials will include database services and may also incorporate reference books or specialized collections of information. If your service is performing telephone research in a narrow niche, your Rolodex may be a critical raw material. If your service is providing space planning, a software package such as AutoCad® may be required. After identifying all the raw materials, list the cost of each. Refer to the product/service planning worksheet at this point (see Figure 7–1 for a completed one).

Separate those items whose cost is based on usage, such as database services, from those with a fixed annual or one-time cost. One-time costs, such as annual fees for database services or the cost of software, are "start-up" costs that will be applied to all products sold in a particular period. Usage-based costs are allocated to individual units. A comprehensive list of materials and costs is essential for correct pricing of the product or service.

The second category of product ingredient is work skills. Indicate your level of competence for each skill. For instance, if your service is to provide literature searches for chemists, the skills would include:

Figure 7–1 Sample Product/Service Planning Worksheet

Product description:

Fixed price trademark searches for software names; package includes Basic Facts About Registering a Trademark from the United States Patent and Trademark Office, (USPTO), and Application for Trademark/Service Mark.

Product ingredients

Resources needed to produce product

Labor/expertise:	Familiarity with trademark databases on LEXIS-NEXIS and facility searching LEXIS-NEXIS and Dialog. Basic understanding of trademark regulations.
Raw materials:	LEXIS-NEXIS, Dialog, CorpTech, Computer Select, USPTO pubs listed above
Packaging:	Folders; form for summary page.
Distribution:	Courier, mail, email, fax.

Cost of resources
Startup costs [subscription fees]: $2650
Resources cost per unit [i.e., per search]: $30–$60

Product life span: Unlimited

Window of opportunity: Unlimited unless PTO makes trademark database available on WWW

Are multiple sales per unit possible: Yes

Target market:

Who is target market:	Small software companies without in-house libraries or legal staff.
Number of potential customers:	5,000
Volume of business/customer expected:	3 per year
Secondary markets:	PR/Advertising firms, attorneys

Figure 7–1 (cont.)

Benefits to customer:

Saves time and cost of filing when name is already in use. Avoids lawsuits. Saves cost of name change. We have resources to provide exceptional common law coverage for software.

Willingness of customer to buy: _____ high __√__ medium _____ low

Value of product to customer: _____ high __√__ medium _____ low

Location of customers: _____ local _____ state __√__ national _____ int'l

Competition

Who are competitors:

FYI in Los Angeles, Thomson & Thomson, Copysearch, Government Liaison Services, The Trademark Register, Trademark Express, attorneys

Advantages/disadvantages of each competitor:

Advantages: Some will file application—we don't

Disadvantages:
FYI: very limited common law search
Others: expensive, common law capability unknown

Ease of market entry: __√__ high _____ medium _____ low

Product awareness of potential customers: _____ high __√__ medium _____ low

- expertise with chemical databases on Dialog, which would include understanding chemical terminology and a familiarity with common processes and classes of chemicals. Dialog resources include Chemical Economics Handbook, Chemical Industry Notes, Chemical Safety Newsbase, Chemstats, Analytical Abstracts.
- expertise with chemical databases on STN International, which includes resources such as Chemical Abstracts, Chemical Engineering Biotechnology Abstracts, CHEMREACT, and so on.

If your skill level is inadequate for any particular item, you have two choices: attend training classes and read instructional materials, or outsource the production segment that requires that skill. For example, a chemical researcher with expertise on Dialog might outsource searches of STN, take a training class, and analyze the output from the STN searcher to acquire the necessary expertise. Or suppose your telephone research skills are weak; consider performing the online portion of research projects and outsourcing any telephone research. In some instances, you can continue to outsource some functions indefinitely, so figure out how important the skill is in producing the product or service. If you design databases for specialized information collections you may occasionally need custom programming. Hiring a programmer may be more practical than learning to program, since programming is only a small segment of the overall system design process.

In evaluating the skills necessary to produce a product, consider the following:

- Do you already have adequate expertise?
- If not, what would be the cost and time required to develop it?
- What portion of the production depends on the skill?
- Are subcontractors available?

If production of the product or service requires several skills that you do not have, it may not be viable to do it. If a critical element requires skills you lack and no one else can perform the work for you, your choice is to develop the skill or abandon the product. Outsourcing is not always an easy answer; you must constantly exercise careful quality control on others' work.

Record your hourly rate for those portions of the process that you will handle on your production ingredients list. Enter the hourly rate of the subcontractors you will employ. If portions of the project will be performed by actual employees, calculate their cost including salary, benefits, FICA, Medicare, unemployment taxes, and workers' compensation insurance.

TARGET MARKET

The next step in the marketing plan is to identify your customers. As with the product definition, the more specific the better. "Medium-sized businesses" is not specific enough. "Public relations and advertising agencies that do not have in-house researchers" is much better. The definition of your customers will dictate how to promote your product.

Next, you have to define the geographic boundaries of your market, since this also affects how you promote your product. If your customers are spread across the country, your advertising strategy will be very different from that for a strictly local market. You may want to plan a local introduction of your service and gradual expansion.

Now you can estimate the size of your market. A larger number of potential customers is not necessarily better than a small number. The ideal size depends on factors such as how much repeat business you can expect from each customer, the amount of the average sale, and your cost to develop the customer in terms of advertising and time.

Some customers need less convincing of the value of your service than others. Public relations and advertising agencies rely heavily on information—it is a major component of their products. Since they normally charge the cost of obtaining information to their clients, those agencies whose clients have deep pockets can spend significant sums on research services. Small agencies that work primarily with small businesses may be more reluctant to pay for information. How much a customer is willing to spend on information is closely related to the customer's perception of how much money he will make or lose based on access to the information. A law firm involved in a multimillion dollar lawsuit will not hesitate to spend vast sums on research. So the strength of your market will depend in large part on the value of your service to your customers and will be a major component in deciding how to price your product.

COMPETITION

Examine the alternate sources for the product or service. If your business provides research, other information brokers—both local firms and large national brokers such as Find/SVP and Teltech—may be competitors. Check your public library's print and CD-ROM resources to see if they, too, would provide nearly equivalent information. Online database vendors promoting user-friendly interfaces for end-user searching are also potential competitors. If your business is to offer consulting services, your competitors will be other consultants and the in-house staff of the client.

Analyze each competitor separately. How does their product differ from yours? What advantages and disadvantages does it offer to the client? What must the client contribute in time and money to the competitor's product? For instance, if your product utilizes data from a government publication that is available on the Internet, why would a client pay for your services rather than access the information himself? The answer may be that your service provides analysis and reformatting that make data instantly usable, whereas a downloaded file from the Internet would require substantial time and effort before the data could be applied to a particular problem. Look back at the description of your product. What value do you add to the raw materials? How do the benefits you give to the client compare with those of your competition? If your product is not obviously better, faster, or more convenient than that of your competitors, it will have to be less expensive.

PRICING YOUR PRODUCT

For services such as on-demand research and consulting, the major cost component is your time. Out-of-pocket expenses may be added, but calculating the cost is primarily a matter of accurate estimating. If your business sells either products or services at a fixed price, however, more complex calculations are needed. If you compile a directory, for instance, then an important step is to determine the cost, in time and other expenses of gathering the data. An additional cost would be the fee charged by a graphic artist to design the layout. These comprise start-up costs (see the product price planning worksheet in Figure 7–2). Based on your analysis of the potential market and the price breaks of the printer (the more copies printed, the less each copy costs), determine the size and cost of the initial printing run. Calculate the amount you would like to make in profit on each volume, and then arrive at an interim price. Although you have not yet figured in the cost of promotion, at this point there is a unit price to compare with the competition's. Whatever amount can be added to the unit cost and still keep the price competitive can be used for promotion. If your preliminary price is already close to that of your competition, consider ways to lower your unit costs or to justify charging a higher price. Review your analysis of the benefits of the product to the clients in the product description and the clients' willingness to spend in your target market profile.

Figure 7–2 Product Price Planning Worksheet

Cost of promotional program: $3,000

Start-up costs (e.g., subscription fees): $2,650

Per unit production cost (average): $50

Per unit profit desired: $50

$$\frac{\$3000 + \$2650}{120 \text{ (\# of units to be sold)}} + \$50 + \$50 = \$150$$

This formula allocates part of the promotion costs and start-up costs to each unit (e.g. directory). These costs, the cost of the actual production, and the profit desired establishes the price.

Consider the product's life cycle. Is the product or service one that will be popular for years, or are you capitalizing on an opportunity that will soon disappear? How many items can be sold to one customer? Customers may purchase a directory of sources in a dynamic industry every year because a substantial amount of new information is included in each edition. Clients whose products require lengthy development time may need a trademark search every few years. Clients who produce several new products each year will need several trademark searches. The price of your product or service will be substantially affected by the speed with which your start-up cost investment must be recouped. If you must sell many units quickly, your promotion costs will be higher. When arriving at a "ballpark" figure for the product's price, plan the promotion of the product then plug the promotion costs into your product price equation. If the cost is not competitive, then modify your promotional plan, which may change your unit sales expectations, which will affect your profit. Several iterations may be required before you arrive at a final price.

PROMOTING YOUR PRODUCT

The goal of promotion is to make potential customers aware of your products and services. If you are promoting a service, your strategy will be very different than if you have a tangible product. In either case, however, begin with the description of your target market. You want to place your company name and your product or service where your target market will see it. To get started, complete a promotional opportunities worksheet, such as the sample in Figure 7–3. The information on the completed worksheet can be used to plan a number of promotional activities—some that require substantial expenditures in money and others that require only time. How you reach your target market will depend not only on the avenues revealed by the worksheet but also on what you plan to sell.

PRINT MEDIA

Industry publications, such as magazines and newsletters, are venues for both paid advertising and free promotion. Paid advertising may be useful if there is a tangible product, such as a book, but it is much less effective for services. To do the job at all, advertising should be placed in publications very narrowly focused at your target market. For example, if your business has compiled a directory of chemical plants indexed by the product manufactured at the location, an ad in *Chemical Marketing Reporter* will have much more impact than one in *Business Week*.

The second essential element for fruitful advertising is repetition. Your first ad will not register unless a reader is actively seeking a directory of chemical plants. After seeing the ad several times, the reader may begin to consider whether such a directory would be useful. As for ad size, in most cases a small ad is less effective than a larger one. Most people will read classified ads only when they are actively looking for a product.

Advertising tends to be expensive. Call those publications that are well targeted to your market and ask for their media kit. Discuss what lead-tracking options they offer, such as an information request card. Find out what products in the same general category as yours have been advertised and ask for a contact name at those companies. For instance, talk with the publisher of a directory of chemists about whether they believe their ad was worth the cost. Ask the periodical's advertising representative for advice on ad size and frequency and what

Figure 7–3 Promotional Opportunities Worksheet

Magazines/newsletters

Name	Publisher	Frequency	Circulation	Focus	Accept advertising?
Software	Sentry Tech	monthly	90,000	Software cos.	yes
Soft-Letter	Soft Letter	biweekly	500	Software developers	no
Structured Progrmg	Springer-Verlag	quarterly	N/A	Software engineers	yes
Sloane Report	Sloane Report	bimonthly	12,000	Software developers	yes
Programmers Jrnl	Programmers Jrnl	bimonthly	40,000	IBM micro programmers	yes
Computer Language	Miller Freeman	monthly	45,000	Programmers	yes
SPA News	SPA	monthly	950	Software publishers	yes

Newspapers

Computer Currents	Computer Crnts	monthly	100,000	Computer users	yes

Radio N/A

Television
Computer Times

Organizations with customers as members

Name	Local chapter?	Meeting schedule
Software Publishers Association	no	—
American Software Association	yes	2nd Tuesday
Independent Computer Consultants Assn	yes	1st Wednesday
Data Processing Management Assn	yes	2nd Thursday

Sources of mailing lists
Software Publishers Association
American Software Association
Soft-Letter
Computer Select
CorpTech

Directories used by customers
Yellow pages
SPA Membership Directory

Listservs and newsgroups
comp.software-eng
comp.windows
comp.programming
insoft-1

assistance you can get on design and layout. If you plan more than a classified ad, you should talk to an advertising agency. Review the rate card for options on size and frequency, and calculate the cost of ad design. Develop costs for several options and insert them into the product price planning worksheet to observe their impact.

If you are promoting a service rather than a product, advertising is probably not a good use of your marketing budget. Most ads cannot provide enough information to generate solid sales leads, whether your business is consulting or research services. From the buyer's point of view, purchasing information services is risky and expensive. Price shopping is nearly impossible; an experienced researcher or consultant can produce a report at a lower overall cost than an inexperienced person, even at a higher hourly rate. The relationship between the quantity of services, their quality, and their cost is unpredictable and difficult to evaluate. In addition, the buyer must share many details on his or her business with the information broker.

Trade publications can, however, be valuable tools in reaching your market, but through their editorial content rather than advertising. If a publication accepts articles from freelance writers, contact the editor and offer to write an article on a subject of interest to the publication's readers—don't make it just a thinly veiled ad, but do include a brief paragraph mentioning your company and location. The article will establish your credentials as an expert and will be in a place potential customers will see your name. (It's sometimes said that a customer must see your name eight times before he or she will initiate a call.)

Generating a mention in a publication that uses only staff writers, or in newspapers, radio, or television, requires more skill. Unless you are personally acquainted with a reporter, you will probably have to start by sending a press release. As with trade publications, there is a greater likelihood of success if you focus your efforts. *American Banker* will be more interested in your specialized research for trust departments than will your hometown daily newspaper. In addition, a mention in *American Banker* will generate calls from many more likely prospects than will an article in the Sunday supplement. Keep in mind that effective marketing requires follow-up. Every call returned takes time, and too many leads at one time can be as unfortunate as none. If you are personally mentioned in an article, be sure you have the resources to respond to inquiries. Calls not returned in a timely manner are leads (and sales) lost.

Before writing your press release, obtain an up-to-date style guide. Press releases that do not follow the conventions will probably be discarded. Remember that reporters are looking for news and for interesting stories, so give your release a "hook" and interesting facts—don't make it just an announcement of your business or description of your service. If your business is promoting your trademark search service, for instance, begin with a statistic on the number of trademark-related lawsuits filed each year. Relate a story about a client who narrowly avoided a disaster through a trademark search. The trick is to include enough information to show a reporter that there is an interesting article to be written on the topic. After sending the press release, follow up. Call the editor of the publication or, for radio or television, the producer of the show. Whenever you call someone in the media, ask if they are "on deadline." If they are, they do not have time to talk and will appreciate your sensitivity. You may well have to make several follow-up calls before an article is written or a segment or interview is scheduled.

MEETING YOUR TARGET MARKET

Because the purchasing decision is so difficult, most sales of information services are made through personal contact between the information broker and the client. Trade and professional organizations can be terrific avenues for reaching those in your target market. A potential client who knows you as an intelligent, considerate, and capable person will find it much easier to use your services than someone who doesn't.

Marketing through organizations requires a substantial commitment in time. First you need to identify likely ones: look for meeting announcements in the newspaper; ask at your public library for lists of local organizations; check the *Encyclopedia of Associations* and similar directories for the national offices of organizations and contact them to see if a local chapter meets in your area. Unless you sell a product or service directly to consumers, most leads/networking groups will not be useful. You want to reach those who can make a decision to purchase your product or service or, at the very least, who can strongly influence the decision. Attend one or two meetings of each potential group and then join those two or three that provide the best contacts. Be sure to restrict the number of groups you join, since attending the meetings is not enough. To use organizations effectively as a marketing vehicle, you must be highly visible. Try to serve as an officer or lead a committee, but do not overcommit. Deliver what you promise, otherwise, your potential clients will not see you as competent or reliable.

Depending on your area of specialization, there may be organizations for your target market whose membership requirements prohibit your joining. The local association of CPAs, for instance, may allow only CPAs to join. In this event, offer them your services as a meeting speaker—a good way to introduce a number of people to your services at one time. However, effective public speaking requires substantial preparation. If you do not have experience in teaching or speaking to groups, look into taking a short course in public speaking. If your target market crosses industry lines, prepare a basic presentation that can be adapted to several target groups. For instance, once you have developed a talk on World Wide Web resources, select specific Web sites of interest to a variety of audiences. Your presentation should highlight your business, but it must also provide interesting information to the audience beyond a recitation of your capabilities. A presentation on the World Wide Web, for example, would reveal the skills a researcher uses and would mention that not all information is available for free on the Web. The ideal presentation should incorporate enough information about your business to provoke questions that allow you to further explain your business. Developing a presentation, even if it can be modified and recycled for various groups, takes significant time. In most cases, you will not be paid for your presentation, so choose a group close enough to your target to be worth the effort.

Carefully consider the number and technological requirements of visual aids when planning your presentation. Some venues may not be able to accommodate live, online demonstrations. The more sophisticated the technology, the greater the potential for complications. If your presentation relies on slides, screen projectors, or online connections, be sure that you are comfortable with the equipment (and that you can provide it), and that your contact at the sponsoring organization is aware of your needs in terms of electrical and telephone connections. Be sure, too, that you can make a reasonably effective presentation if everything fails.

Whatever the nature of your presentation, it must fit the time allotted. A hurried presentation will not be effective, so don't pack too much information in a short time. Your audience should leave with a little enlightenment about the basic topic, some understanding of your business, and an impression of you as a competent and knowledgeable person. High-quality handouts in the form of brochures, bibliographies, lists of resources, and the like, are essential. They give your audience something to take home to remember you and your business by. Put your company name and telephone number on every handout.

Once you have developed a presentation, you need exert only a little more effort to turn it into an article. The article can reinforce the presentation if it is included in the newsletter of the sponsoring organization, or, if scheduling a presentation is a problem, the article can substitute for the presentation. Develop several versions of the article, focusing on specific audiences and varying the length and tone to fit different types of publications. The article may serve to attract interest in the presentation. Be sure that your name, company name, and contact information are included at the beginning or end of the article.

DIRECT MAIL

Like advertising, direct mail is expensive and requires careful selection of your target market. Your first step is to identify a suitable mailing list. Reasonably high quality mailing lists are available from associations. Lists are also available from trade magazines, but they include libraries and individuals who may have only a peripheral interest in your product or service. Watch out for mailing lists from publications that rely on "qualification" cards rather than payment from subscribers; they will have a higher percentage of out-of-date names and addresses.

After selecting the list, prepare the mailer. As with advertising, direct mail is more effective for a tangible product. Unlike advertising, however, it does put something in the potential customer's hand that may be retained. Even a customer without a current interest in your service may keep a brochure for possible future use. Brochures that incorporate a business card are particularly good for this purpose, and now you can even print them on your laser or ink-jet printer, allowing you to print small batches.

Whether printing your own or having them printed, seek professional design help for both the format and text of the brochure. Most people without advertising expertise put far too much information in the brochure, focusing on the features of their product or service and too little on the benefits. Features and credentials should be included, but they are secondary. Research clients, for instance, are less interested in the number of databases that can be accessed than in the fact that you can save them time. So have a professional design your first brochure; you can revise it as needed in the future. Contact several small advertising agencies; find someone whose work for other clients appeals to you and who will take the time to understand your business and how your clients will benefit from your services. You can even suggest a barter arrangement: trade your research time for the brochure designer's time; most ad agencies need research, but a small agency may not be able to afford it. Calculate the cost of the mailing list, the brochure design, printing and postage, and enter it into the product price planning worksheet. Then calculate the amount you must sell to recoup your promotional costs.

Keep in mind that direct mail, on average, generates *inquiries* from less than 2 percent of recipients. You can increase the response rate from direct mail by sending small mailings at weekly intervals and following up with telephone calls. To be effective, however, you must be persistent enough to get past receptionists and secretaries, and you must be able to accept rejection. If you hate talking to strangers or are a reluctant salesperson, you probably will not make those all-important follow-up calls. In that case, your promotional budget would be better spent elsewhere.

Although direct mail may not gain many new clients, it can be effective in generating repeat business from current clients. As your client list grows, so will your mailing list. In some cases, it may be possible to supplement your own mailing list with names from others. Mail out postcards on a regular basis to remind clients of your existence, or start a regular newsletter, which can also educate your clients on how your services can help them, alert them to new service and product offerings, and contribute to your image as an expert. If you lack either the time or expertise to write a newsletter, F1 Services, Inc. (www.netcom.com/~f1srvcs), provides articles that you can format and reproduce.

DIRECTORY LISTINGS

Perhaps the most effective means of promotion for service businesses is directory listings. Customers who find your business through a directory are "prequalified"—they have already determined that they need the services your business provides. (If your business is listed under "Information Brokers," the customer has probably been referred by a librarian or other information professional, since information broker is still a relatively unfamiliar term.) To be effective, advertising must be seen by the prospect when he or she is ready to buy, and directories are a readily available source of information for potential clients. Some directories, such as those published by Gale Research, will list your company at no charge, but you will usually pay a fee to be listed in directories that are distributed free. Call the directory publisher for forms and information on the subscriber base.

Study directories to be certain section headings are descriptive and appropriate to your business. If your business is listed under a heading that is too broad, you may spend time responding to numerous unproductive inquiries. In determining the size of your listing, consider the number of competitors in the directory, the sizes of other listings, and how closely the recipients of the directory match your target market. If a directory is focused specifically on your market and contains listings for several of your key competitors, you will probably want a substantial listing, since customers tend to assume that companies with good-sized directory listings are more established and larger than those with smaller listings.

A key directory is your local telephone company's Yellow Pages. To be included, your business must have a business telephone line. In many cities, residential and business telephone listings are separated, but a business telephone line will get you a free listing in the business White Pages as well as the Yellow Pages. If your primary business is research, your business should be listed under the headings "Information Brokers" or "Information Search and Retrieval Services." If your Yellow Pages do not currently include such a heading, request that it be added. Support your case by using other directories such as the AIIP membership directory and *Burwell Directory of Information Brokers* to identify other businesses in your area that would likely advertise under the "Information Brokers" heading if it were available. Do not list your business under "Library Research Services" or any other heading containing the word "library" unless your clients are libraries. Research clients tend to associate the word "library" with free information. If your business is listed under a broad category such as "Consulting," be sure your listing includes a tagline that identifies your specific niche, such as "space planning for libraries and information centers." Likewise, if you have a listing under "Market Research" but your business provides only secondary research, insert a line that indicates that limitation. Explaining to callers that you do not do surveys wastes your time as well as theirs. If your clients are geographically diverse, it may be important to invest in a toll-free number and listings in several Yellow Pages directories.

THE WORLD WIDE WEB

With the rapid growth of the Internet and the World Wide Web, it makes sense to create a business presence on the Internet. The place to start is to design a "home page," which is basically an introductory screen that can be accessed by prospective clients and existing customers via the Internet. The home page, along with the other "pages" of information designed in HTML (HyperText Markup Language), constitute your Web presence. The typical home page uses highlighted images, or hypertext, that lead the user more deeply into specific topics or subjects. The Internet allows for the use of customized graphics and sound and video capabilities to present yourself and your company.

Design your Web services for those who are likely to access the service. Your home page should incorporate a menu that guides prospective clients and other "visitors" to information, and other pathways that lead your customer to services such as ordering search updates or publications.

The effectiveness of Internet Web pages as a marketing and business tool depends on whether your prospective clients "surf," what type of products your business offers, and how well the home page is designed, maintained, and updated. If your business service is selling books or publishing a newsletter, the home page may be reasonably effective. If your business primarily provides customized research services, a Web page will probably not bring in significant business since those who have time to find your home page probably do much of their own research. But if you are presenting your company as one that utilizes the latest in information technology, be sure to include a Web address on your business card.

A home page can also be quite useful for distributing your marketing packet. Writing cover letters and gathering and mailing the elements of your information package can be amazingly time consuming. With a home page, you can simply refer any "wired" prospects to your home page and let them download the information.

A home page may be the first exposure potential customers have to your business, so its design must be effective and appropriate. The three most important elements in Web page design are:

- effective content: your home page should contain material sought by those who will access your page. Design your home page to guide potential customers who may be "browsing" to see what your business has to offer, and to guide existing clients to specific services.
- effective design: pages should be interesting, pleasing to look at, and satisfying to the customer. The average "hit" to a Web page lasts a mere six seconds, so your pages should look good enough to hold a visitor's interest.
- efficient navigation: design access so customers and users do not have to make multiple steps to access important information.

If you have the necessary expertise, consider setting up and operating your own home page. But if you feel you do not have the necessary skills or time to devote to this project, then use a contractor for home page design and Web server set-up. Before designing your own page, examine the home pages of others and determine which work well and why. Visit the Commercial Sites Directory (www.directory.net) to view thousands of home pages.

Incorporate these features in your home page:

- graphics—but not ones that take a long time to download
- brief descriptions—but provide links to more complex material
- navigational signals about how to get around.

Internet economics are such that it may be more cost effective to lease space from an Internet provider for your home page than to mount your own page on your business server. Using the Internet service provider's (ISP) home page address may be a better solution, particularly if the vendor will maintain your links and connections to other Web pages and regularly update your home page for you. Use care in selecting an ISP, however (see Figure 7–4). Changing your e-mail address and home page location becomes expensive once your e-mail and URL address are incorporated on your business cards and in your marketing and promotional materials.

There are now sufficient Internet service providers to cover the whole of the United States and to provide some price and service competition. Some providers offer nationwide service, such as EarthLink or NETCOM, which you can access via an 800 number connection; other ISPs focus on local markets at the state or local level. Find telephone listings for ISPs in the Yellow Pages under "Computers—Online Services" and "Internet," or pick up a copy of a local computing magazine, newsletter, or user-group publication that carries ads and information on local ISPs.

You can also use the Internet as a promotional vehicle by participating in selected listservs and newsgroups. But be extremely careful in your postings. If you provide answers to questions, keep your tone friendly and nonpatronizing; you want to be viewed as an expert but not a know-it-all. Avoid anything that sounds like advertising—newsgroup participants are very sensitive to self-promotion or postings that resemble broadcast mailings. Your reputation will be established as those in your target market see your name in several venues.

Looking to the future, you might want eventually to consider building video-conferencing capabilities. Currently the most reasonable is CU See Me, which was developed at Cornell University and is available as a freeware product. Otherwise you can obtain a commercial version from White Pine Software for $99 (www.goliath.wpine.com). The quality, however, will not be high; if you want more quality consider MPEG-1, which provides full-screen VHF quality.

Figure 7–4 Selecting an Internet Service Provider

Customer Support

Does the ISP provide 24–hour support and service?
Does the ISP have a toll-free help line?
Does the ISP have experience with companies of your size?

Redundancy

Does the ISP have multiple host computers operating to provide continuous service?
Does the ISP have multiple connections to the Internet backbone with T-1 lines?

Platform support

Does the ISP support different access methods including PPP, SLIP, and ISDN?

Services

Does the ISP provide World Wide Web (WWW) and Hypertext Transport Protocol (HTTP) Service?
Does the ISP provide Domain Name Service (DNS) and backup?
Does the ISP support Post Office Protocol (POP) e-mail?
Does the ISP provide Usenet service?
How many Usenets are supported?
Does the ISP provide Network News Transfer Protocol (NNTP) for accessing newsgroups?
Does the ISP provide WWW server capability for creating and hosting your Web pages?

Source: Ford 1997.

FOLLOWING THROUGH

Regardless of the promotion techniques you choose, they are only the first step. Unless you sell a tangible product, promotion produces only leads, not sales. If you do not respond to inquiries, you waste both your time and money. As your business grows, you may need to hire temporary clerical help to respond to sudden surges of interest. And don't neglect leads simply because you currently have enough business; spend at least eight hours every week on marketing. Small businesses often experience a feast or famine sales cycle—entrepreneurs initially spend significant time on marketing but do none when business picks up. At the end of a contract or busy period (and they always do end), they then must spend time marketing with little business to support them.

SETTING AN IMAGE

Despite the dramatic increase in the number of companies involved in selling information services, few people are aware of what most information brokers do. Often information brokers are confused with private investigators. Or an individual may have read an article on a particular broker in a narrow specialization and assumes you provide the same services. It is important that you establish an identity for your company and that you develop a concise, appealing way to describe your service.

Establishing your company identity means defining a corporate image. The high turnover rate in the industry has given the information-services profession a somewhat "fly-by-night" image. To counter this, you want to establish an image of reliability. Always return calls, and check for messages frequently when you are out of your office.

To respond to leads, you will need a high-quality package of marketing materials. The marketing packet is one of the key tools for establishing your company's identity and your corporate image. Presentation is important in establishing not only your corporate image but also the validity of the information provided. A pleasant, easy-to-read font, laser printing, and an attractive binding will support this goal. The package should include a description of the benefits of your service to clients, biographical information on the principals, information on how charges are calculated, and invoicing procedures. Your package may consist of materials in letter format, or you may want a brochure. If you publish a newsletter for your clients, you should enclose it as well.

All your marketing materials should promote a consistent company image. Information services are not an impulse purchase, so consistency in your style is an important design consideration. Your choice of stationery and business cards, the message on your answering machine, your brochures, the location of your office, if you have one, and the presentation format of your research reports should spark recognition and reinforce your corporate image. The impression your clients and potential clients have of your company is formed by every contact.

Answer your telephone with a businesslike but friendly greeting and tone. When you meet with clients, dress like the successful business person you hope to be. If you work out of your home, be sure that background noises such as dogs and children cannot be heard over your telephone conversations. Many telephone companies offer a voice-mail service that routes callers to voice mail when your line is busy, which is preferable to "call waiting." Clients should be aware that they are not your only customer, but should be treated as if they were. Record a concise voice-mail message. If you must have a lengthy message, give callers the option of bypassing it and leaving a message without listening to the end.

REVIEW AND REVISE

Attempt to track how prospective clients learned of your service. When a call comes in, always ask, "How did you hear about us?" When an ad or directory listing is up for renewal, you should have some data on which to base your renewal decision. If your business receives leads from a mention in a newspaper or magazine article or from an article you have written, track how many of the leads turn into actual customers. Code your brochures or put a code in the return address so you can track responses. If you send out hundreds of information packets and receive very little work from that group, it may be a good idea to avoid that publication in the future. On the other hand, if a direct-mail campaign was particularly effective, consider sending additional mailings to the same list.

Products and product lines evolve, and a publication on a hot topic may have a shelf life of only one year. So if sales for a particular product decline over several months, the product may not be reaching the end of its life cycle but may simply need a promotional boost. Consider reducing the price, trying a new promotional technique, or completely eliminating promotion for the product to reduce costs.

Review your products and services, and their markets, every four to six months. If you originally expected that clients for your trademark search would be software companies, but in the last four months all the new calls have been from attorneys, consider adjusting your promotional plan. As your client base builds, you should obtain basic data that allow you to analyze the market as it really is, as opposed to what you assumed it would be. The demographics you track in your client database should include location, size of company, line of business, origin of lead, and products/services purchased. Elaborate statistical analysis is not necessary, but the data should help you determine the nature of your markets for each product or service. It should also help you know if sales are increasing or declining, and whether each product/service is profitable. Adjust your marketing plan and take advantage of what you have learned about your market.

SOURCES

CITED IN TEXT

Joe Ford and Associates, Inc. *Automation for Libraries: A Quarterly Report of John Ford and Associates* (Vol. 2, No. 1), January 1997, p. 1.

FOR FURTHER INFORMATION

Check directories such as the *Thomas Register of American Manufacturers, Rand McNally Commercial Atlas and Marketing Guide, Standard Rate and Data Service, Encyclopedia of Associations,* and *Directories in Print* to find clients. You can find copies of these directories at your local library.

Join your local Toastmasters, speaking bureau, and other clubs. Check for listings in the telephone Yellow Pages or contact your local Chamber of Commerce, community college, or economic development center.

Direct-mailing services for bulk and promotional mailings can be located in your telephone directory under "Mailing Lists" and "Mailing Services." Mailing lists can be obtained from many publishers. Check the reference sections of your library's business department for current lists of mailing-list brokers, which will give information on sizes and types of lists that are available.

8 THE RESPONSIBLE BROKER

Information brokers make a profit from providing information services. The independent nature of their work means that information brokers—like accountants, psychologists, and social workers—are likely to be called upon to make judgments that are unique, uncertain, equivocal, or have the potential for conflicts of interest. On a day-to-day basis, you may find your routine dominated by practical problems of meeting deadlines, maintaining the flow of work, and soliciting new clients and business, yet it is important that you be vigilant in maintaining the highest professional and personal standards in the conduct of your work and your business activities. Be vigilant to dilemmas hidden in daily routines and practices that are unfair or compromise personal or societal values such as privacy or intellectual freedom. Striving for ethical decision making will help improve the quality of your decisions and help you avoid making poor decisions. Poor decisions have practical consequences: they can damage social and business relationships between people, lose customers, or lead to legal proceedings. In addition, it is important to demonstrate ethical behavior and make your clients aware that you follow ethical principles because information brokers do not have an established reputation. Every broker who does a bad job or behaves in an unethical manner subtracts from the potential market for all brokers. A client who has been disappointed by an information broker will tell others.

CODES OF ETHICS AND CONDUCT

One way to learn about ethical behavior and to begin to establish a personal code for yourself is to examine the various ethical codes that already exist. Since information brokers occupy a unique niche as service providers, it is important to familiarize yourself with a number of codes that speak to developing ethical, personal, professional, and business practices.

Some codes relevant to information brokers include that of the Association of Independent Information Professionals (AIIP) and the Code of Ethics for Librarians. A number of more comprehensive, professional ethical codes, such as the Code of Ethics of the American Society for Information Science (ASIS) may also be worth reviewing. (Appendix D contains copies of these codes.) Professional codes are handy guides to key issues such as: the importance of being competent in the execution of your duties; adhering to moral and legal standards; adopting standards for making public statements; preserving confidentiality; showing interest in the welfare of the customer; and developing and maintaining technical and specialized knowledge. As your business develops you may wish to adapt and adopt a formal code of conduct for your own business.

You can also access useful information about ethical practices from the various information industry codes for fair business and credit practices; from legal statutes and laws, including the Privacy Act of 1974; and from recent legislation on electronic systems and consumer privacy. The Data Processing Managers Association Code and the Association for Computing Machinery (ACM) Code are also good sources of information about ethical principles.

A DECISION-MAKING GUIDE

Ethical decisions are part of the overall management responsibilities for information brokers, but sometimes it is hard to determine whether an ethical issue has arisen or not. The following short set of questions (adapted from Lewis 1991, 106) should help you determine whether you are confronted with a situation that presents ethical problems:

1. Is this really an ethical issue? Am I confused about what to do, or am I afraid to do what is right?
2. Who else is involved in this situation, and who else will be affected by my decision?
3. Have I caused this problem or has someone else; is it my problem to solve?
4. What are the ethical duties involved, legal obligation, fairness, respect, avoiding harm?
5. What do others think?
6. Would another broker act in the same manner, and what will others think of my decision?

GETTING AND KEEPING SECRETS

The most important and challenging relationship is that which exists between the broker and the client. Information brokers function as consultants to their clients in the same manner as therapists or management consultants. Your role is to work with the client in order to define a problem that you are expected to solve through the provision of information services. These relationships demand that you adopt the highest standards of conduct.

Central to the broker/client relationship is its confidential nature. Never reveal a client's request. There is no law that says that information brokers are obligated to keep secrets for clients, but it is ethically important to do so. All ethical codes hold that the transactions that occur between the client and the professional are special, private, and confidential. The information broker must observe in his or her actions the primacy of the welfare of the client. The ethical principal is that of harm minimization, or the "first do no harm" concept. Upholding this basic principle, however, can cause conflict between values in certain circumstances. Suppose a client is paying for research in technical fields that the client feels can be sold to a foreign county for a profit, even if the sale of this form of technology is illegal. Do you have a responsibility to maintain confidentiality with the client, or should you report this transaction? At least one writer has argued that violating client confidentiality may be permitted in cases wherein serious harm is to be avoided (Woodward 1990). The general rule should be to protect client confidentiality unless there is clear and sufficient evidence that the breach of confidentiality would be warranted in order to achieve a greater benefit or avoid creating greater harm.

ACTING RESPONSIBLY

One specific impact of the ubiquitous computer has been an escalation in the awareness that, to be competitive, American business must engage in active, ongoing, strategic and tactical information gathering—defined generally as organizational intelligence. Information brokers with business clients are accustomed to research requests on competitors' products, but the search for competitive information can pose ethical dilemmas. If you do online research, never recycle your research results to another client or maintain them for another use. This is considered a violation of copyright laws. Publishers and database producers are very sensitive about copyright, partly because technology makes it so easy to violate.

The case of the internal, corporate-telephone directories illustrates the "hidden" nature of some ethical dilemmas. As the story was reported in the *Information Advisor* (n.d.), the editor of this newsletter spotted an ad for a business that was collecting, photocopying, and selling corporate internal phone directories. The editor contacted the president of this new telephone directory company, who stated that he felt there was nothing wrong with this practice but admitted that the company had obtained its directories in a manner—from temporary employees and "other means"—that avoided having to ask the company for them directly. Although it was not clear whether copyright laws were being violated, this information may be "proprietary," which means that it is not in the public domain and is not readily accessible by anyone publicly. Is it ethical for the information broker to purchase such a directory service even knowing that the means by which this information was obtained was less than forthright? To the credit of the newsletter editor, the editor questioned the ethics of purchasing this source and advocated pursuing other research alternatives, such as calling the company directly, to obtain a company or employee fact book.

Do not gather information using illegal means, and do not get information from others whom you suspect may use illegal means. Be aware that if you obtain information from someone who has gotten it illegally—for example, by asking a friend on the police force to check a national crime database—you can be charged with the same crime as the person who got it for you, something that has happened to information brokers in the past. In addition, and for the same reasons, be careful about using subcontractors. Make it your business to know something about them and their reputation.

Do not misrepresent yourself or lie to your information sources. Trying to obtain information about competitors makes it tempting for an information broker to claim to be a graduate student, or to sweet-talk unsuspecting secretaries and librarians. Don't do it. Tell the source you are a research firm. If your client wants you to get proprietary information by dissembling, tell them to do their own research, and tell the client why you are unwilling to misrepresent yourself.

ACTING COMPETENTLY

These days, there are greatly expanded choices in selecting formats and information sources to meet the needs of clients. Your decisions about what is fair and correct for the client should be based upon a knowledge of the client's needs, but should also include an assessment of the client's ability to pay.

Above all, it is important to exhibit professionalism in knowledge and demeanor. You have a responsibility to master the complex body of knowledge that comprises your domain of practice. If you find you are beyond your depth of expertise in a certain area, don't claim you have it anyway; instead, turn the research over to a broker who specializes in that subject area.

Do not charge clients for your mistakes. If you make a stupid mis-take on a search, do not bill the client and expect the client to pay for it. Some projects may be learning experiences, and when you finish there may be a lot you would do differently the second time around. But don't take advantage of your clients by learning your job at their expense. This is particularly challenging for brokers who practice in a rapidly developing and evolving technical and commercial realm. The prudent broker will take steps to ensure the client receives accurate information from up-to-date sources and to conduct the search appropriately. At this time there does not appear to be a set standard to define "reasonable care," so brokers have to rely upon the codes of ethics and limitations of liability to protect themselves in this area.

Keep in mind that your choices of information sources can have the potential for adverse effects if the information is inaccurate or out-of-date, the use of which could cause the client harm (Mintz 1991). Prudent brokers typically utilize limited liability statements or disclaimers that state that their ability to verify the accuracy of a source is limited. The statement alerts the client that possible errors may be present despite the caution exercised by the broker in selecting and using a specific source.

MATCHING CLIENT EXPECTATIONS

Brokers must take care that their ability to perform work is equivalent to the expectations of the client. It is unethical to misrepresent your qualifications and the ability of your firm to produce a product or service in a timely or competent manner. Ethically you should have the education and background to perform the work requested by the client. As an information broker, it is not responsible behavior to "learn on the job" after representing to the client that you know how to perform the requested research and have the necessary skills and resources to carry it out.

OPERATING AN ETHICAL ORGANIZATION

As an employer and principal of a firm, hire qualified employees and be sure that employees receive appropriate training and educational opportunities to keep abreast of the latest information sources. Guard against misrepresenting, being dishonest, or being defensive about an employee's mistakes or capabilities when questioned by a client. Failure to ensure that research is performed by a qualified employee can have a negative impact on a firm's future outlook. For instance, there was a lawsuit filed against Dun & Bradstreet after sloppy research by a sixteen-year-old summer intern provided inaccurate information about a company that was included in D&B's Business Information Report database (Froelich 1992). It is ethically responsible for an information broker to make restitution to a client, such as refunding search costs, if the data are incorrect as a direct result of the broker's error.

As a business owner and as an information professional, you have a responsibility to ensure your own employees act in an ethical manner. Be sure to introduce employees to industry and professional codes and expect employees to honor these standards of conduct in their work. The Code of Ethical Business Practice prepared by the Association of Independent Information Professionals, the ACM Code of Ethics and Professional Conduct, and the ASIS Professional Guidelines all have statements relevant to the work performed by brokers.

MAINTAINING AN INDEPENDENT ATTITUDE

Exercise independence and objectivity in selecting tools and services on behalf of the client. As an information broker, you will have a complex relationship with publishers and database vendors regarding your sense of responsibility to report any concerns about source accuracy should they occur. Since you are using their services to operate a private business and to generate a profit, you must abide by licenses and regulations that restrict you from repackaging or reselling information without prior authorization.

Guard against improper influence by vendors. If you rely upon one vendor's service or products because of favorable prices or discounts, you may be acting unethically by placing your benefit ahead of that of the client. As the diversity and complexity of information formats, sources, and services increase, avoid building sole-source relationships with vendors that may be comfortable for you but that do not necessarily serve the client's needs. Be ethically responsible, and take actions and make decisions based upon the merits of the product.

As the information environment has become more complex in terms of sources—with an array of print, online, CD-ROM, and Internet-accessible sources—and format choices, it has also become more competitive. There may be the temptation to accept inducements and incentives to use certain sources. This could be a conflict of interest and unethical as well.

GUARDING INTELLECTUAL PROPERTY

Information is property and must be safeguarded appropriately when it is in your care. Such fiduciary relationship extends to taking precautions to block unauthorized access to proprietary databases as well as exercising vigilance against fire, theft, or computer-virus attacks that can damage data and data systems owned by you or a client.

Protect information as intellectual property. Copyright violations, software piracy, and unauthorized use of artwork offer strong arguments that information brokers adopt ethically responsible positions to prevent them.

The question of who owns information is becoming a problem of "wicked" proportions; there are intertwined legal and ethical issues based on questions of who is the author, who is the publisher, and who pays for information. Copyright law has rested on the dual principles of recognizing the right of the creator to be compensated for the production of an intellectual product, and the somewhat contradictory principle of "Fair Use," which acknowledges the right of individuals to copy a portion of a work so long as the copied item is intended for personal use and does not result in gain to the user.

UPHOLDING LICENSES AND AGREEMENTS

Act in an honest and trustworthy manner with clients, suppliers, and vendors. At some point you may find yourself purchasing hardware, software, and services from another party. To obtain these services, you will be obliged to sign some type of contract or agreement that states the obligations and duties of each party.

A classic example of how clear such a contract can appear and how difficult it can be to implement is illustrated by a situation not uncommon to many of us who depend upon computers to perform our work. You have paid personally for a microcomputer software package to use at work. The license agreement for the product states you may install and use the package on a "single machine." Since your business is a sole proprietorship, you also want to work at home. You are sure you will be the only person using the package at any given time, both at home and at work, and therefore feel it is permissible to install the software on both machines. Is it? These questions raise ethical as well as legal questions that are still being debated.

Online vendors control their information and services through license provisions. Brokers must lease or use database resources under the conditions set out by the database owner and must abide by license provisions. You must exercise care to ensure that license provisions are understood and adhered to in searching, formatting, and providing reports of database materials to clients. Different database suppliers have various levels of permissions and licensing requirements that define formatting, downloading, copying, and storing information. Some suppliers permit temporary storage of search results; others limit or restrict searches to be offered to the original or requesting client only, no reselling permitted. Policies and practices vary among vendors, so be aware of them and agree to abide by the agreements set by the vendors.

The following guidelines developed for online searchers capture many of the key issues and problems of the broker's relationships with database and information suppliers/vendors, as contrasted with their responsibilities to the client.

The information broker has a responsibility to:

- maintain awareness of the range of information sources available in a given area in order to best serve the client.
- ensure the selection of a database and system by the information broker is not biased due to familiarity with the source as opposed to being based upon the client needs.
- disclose to the client the limitations of the database or system in meeting the client's needs.
- indicate to the client any concerns regarding accuracy or inclusiveness of the database or system which may affect search outcomes (Mintz 1991).

MAINTAINING RELATIONSHIPS WITH PUBLIC INSTITUTIONS

There is often tension between information brokers and professional librarians. Some librarians believe the information broker's client is getting a "better deal" from the public institution than the off-the-street public. Be sensitive to the fact that some professionals within those institutions feel that the information broker unfairly exploits public-information sources to create private gain and profit. The Association of Independent Information Professionals' (AIIP) Code of Ethical Business Practice recognizes this tension and recommends that brokers be scrupulous in not unreasonably or unfairly monopolizing the resources of a public institution, such as asking for special favors, exploiting a friendship with a certain professional in a particular institution, engaging in extended spells of photocopying while others wait in line, and the like. Avoid even the appearance of unfair or unequal advantage gained by the client through his or her access to the information broker.

EMERGING ISSUES

Your practice is likely to be affected by the rapid changes accompanying the digitization of data and the growth in size and extent of large national and international electronic data systems. The availability and accessibility of personal information is growing rapidly. As an information broker, you may be asked by clients to conduct searches of personal data as these sources become commercially available and accessible. Be prepared to respond to clients, to explain whether you provide these services, and under what conditions. It is your responsibility to use personal data carefully and to understand the source and limitations to this type of data.

Internet access offers benefits, but it also carries risks. Not long ago, a Connecticut illustrator found his work was being scanned, digitally altered, and distributed freely over the Internet without his knowledge (Roberts 1993). The practice resulted in hundreds of individuals and companies making use of copyrighted material without compensation to the creator. The illustrator sued and successfully collected damages from the online company that distributed his images. This raises some good questions worthy of consideration. How likely is it that you may unknowingly use someone's intellectual property without proper authorization and agreement? How likely is it someone will accuse you of stealing from them? To avoid painful consequences, maintain careful records and controls over the sources of materials such as art work appearing on the Internet and from other electronic sources. There are rules and laws that protect intellectual property; so if you're thinking about copying material but it is not clear who owns the copyright, don't do it. All users of the new electronic technologies should recommit themselves to the basic rules of conduct and apply the same standards they would use in dealing with intellectual property in print form.

A CHECKLIST OF ETHICAL CONCERNS

Given the prescriptions and precepts of ethical conduct, how can you exercise practical ethical behavior? The following list is intended as a starting point for practitioners interested in integrating an ethical approach into their business activities.

DEVELOP STANDARDS FOR PERSONAL CONDUCT

Observe the basic moral responsibilities of caring, honesty, accountability, keeping promises, pursuit of excellence, loyalty, fairness, integrity, respect for others, and responsible citizenship as part of your basic personal and business behavior.

Read and understand the code(s) of ethics statements on personal conduct.

Use commonsense tests for examining your conduct in given situations:

- The "Mom" test—can you tell her what you did, and will she approve?
- The "Other Person's Shoes" test—if the roles were reversed, would you feel the same way about the situation?

DEFINE THE CLIENT RELATIONSHIP

Regard all matters discussed with clients as confidential and private.

Accept work from clients only after determining that you and your firm are able to meet time deadlines and perform the work accurately, efficiently, and effectively, using the most appropriate sources.

Disclose to clients limitations, conditions, or aspects of your services that alter or affect the service you offer to the client.

Disclose to the client through the use of a disclaimer that all work performed is subject to the condition and adequacy of the databases and systems used in the search, and disclose the limits of your responsibility for the services performed.

Undertake services that limit data collection to published and publicly available sources of information only.

Sign and honor any nondisclosure agreements whereby you keep confidential any sensitive information.

INCORPORATE ETHICAL CONCERNS INTO ORGANIZATIONAL RELATIONSHIPS

Consider retaining liability insurance—an essential item if there is an office location and additional employees at the broker's location.

Examine and verify the educational credentials of your employees.

Ensure you and your employees keep technically current by attending professional meetings and educational and training sessions.

Take responsibility for employee quality, and acknowledge and provide reparation when necessary for errors in the data through downloading or reformatting.

CLARIFY RELATIONSHIPS WITH VENDORS AND SUPPLIERS

Understand and observe all licenses and agreements with vendors, and understand the provisions under which you may act as a third-party information searcher for your client.

Ensure that sources and systems used to produce searches and information are as current and accurate as comparable products in the marketplace.

Understand and observe copyright provisions and pay copyright fees when appropriate.

Avoid accepting gifts, endorsements, monetary discounts, or other favors that may create disproportionate loyalty toward a vendor and/or have the appearance of conflict of interest.

CREATE AN ETHICAL ENVIRONMENT

Examine the relevant legal legislation on privacy as it relates to your business and professional practices.

Stay up on current issues related to social computing, credit, and personal-data reporting and their impact on your business.

Observe basic rules of courtesy and good manners at all times when interacting with individuals through electronic networks and services.

In the course of running your business, you will be faced with ethical decisions that never occurred to you. To better anticipate such situations consider the scenarios on page 112.

Following the advice in this section and adopting the guidelines will help you take the first steps toward developing standards of ethical conduct to guide your business relationships. Doing so, however, is not a "quick fix," but rather a process and a set of techniques to improve decision making under conditions where there are few rules and many conditions of uncertainty as to the best course of action. As a responsible broker, you should attempt to incorporate the principles of ethical behavior into your daily working life and exercise your ethical decision making regularly so it becomes part of doing things right and doing the right thing.

SAMPLE ETHICAL ISSUES

A client explains his company's future expansion plans in the course of requesting research. You are later asked by a second client to provide a competitive analysis of the first company. What should you do?

Two advertising agencies ask for background on the same company that is soliciting bids for its advertising account. Should you tell your clients you are working for both of the agencies?

A client asks for everything that can be found on a company in which he plans to invest, but is only willing to spend $250. How do you advise the client about what you are willing to do?

A client wants pricing information from his competitors and has asked you to call them and say you are a potential customer.

A client has asked you to recommend a library automation system. You recommend one from which you receive a "finder's fee" even though it is not really the best package for the client's situation.

A client asks for the most recently published articles on a topic from industry newsletters. You neglect to advise him that there is a three-week embargo on the newsletters before they are available online. Is it your responsibility to inform the client of this fact?

A client asks for a "clean copy" of an article so he can make copies to hand out to clients. What should you tell the client?

You are a part-time student, so you use your "educational" password to search databases for clients. Is this ethical and legal?

A client asks you to obtain the "missing pages" from his copy of another company's internal telephone directory. Should you obtain this information for the client?

SOURCES

CITED IN TEXT

Froehlich, T. J. "Ethical Considerations of Information Professionals." *Annual Review of Science and Technology (ARIST)* 27 (1992): 291–324.

Lewis, Carol. *The Ethics Challenge in Public Service.* San Francisco: Jossey-Bass, 1991, p. 106.

Mintz, Anne. "Ethics and the News Librarian." *Special Libraries* 82(1) (1991): 10.

Roberts, P. "Electronic Ethics." *Aldus Magazine* (June 1993):15–18.

Woodward, Diane. "A Framework for Deciding Issues in Ethics." *Information Ethics Concerns for Librarianship and the Information Industry*, ed. Anne Mintz. Jefferson, NC: McFarland, 1990, pp. 4–23.

FOR FURTHER INFORMATION

Many professional associations publish their codes of ethics. These are a few that can provide copies of codes (some of these appear in Appendix D):

The American Library Association, 50 East Huron Street, Chicago, Illinois 60611, phone: (312) 944–6780.

American Society for Information Science, 8720 Georgia Avenue, Suite 501, Silver Spring, MD 20910, phone: (301) 495–0900.

The Special Libraries Association, 1700 18th Street NW, Washington, DC 20009, phone: (202) 234–4700.

The Internet has Web sites that provide information on ethics and privacy:

The Electronic Frontier Foundation (www.eff.org)

The Electronic Privacy Information Center (www.epc.org/privacy/privacyresources.frq.html)

Privacy Rights Clearinghouse (www.privacyrights.org)

APPENDIX A: SELECTED ONLINE DATABASE SERVICES

Burrelle's Broadcast Database
75 East Northfield Road
Livingston, NJ 07039
(800) 631–1160
www.burrelles.com
(Transcripts of television programs)

CompuServe Information Service
5000 Arlington Centre Boulevard
Columbus, OH 43220
(800) 848–8990
www.compuserve.com
(Menu driven, over 500 databases including games and special group
bulletin boards)

Data-Star
2440 W. El Camino Real
Mountain View, CA 94090
(800) 334–2564
www.products.dialog.com/products/datastarweb
(Concentration on European business and biomedical information)

Dialog Corporation
2440 West El Camino Real
Mountain View, CA 94040
(800) 334–2564
www.dialog.com
(Over 400 databases, concentration on business information)

Dow Jones Interactive
Dow Jones & Company, Inc.
PO Box 300
Princeton, NJ 08543–0300
(800) 369–7466
www.djinteractive.com
(Full-text databases covering business and investments)

Information America
600 West Peachtree Street, Suite 1200
Atlanta, GA 30308
(800) 235–4008
www.infoam.com
(Public records)

Information Resource Service Company
3777 North Harbor Boulevard
Fullerton, CA 92835
(800) 640–4772
www.irsc.com
(Public records)

Investext
Thomson Financial Networks
11 Farnsworth Street
Boston, MA 02210
(800) 662–7878
www.investext.com
(Full text of brokerage reports, market research reports)

LEXIS-NEXIS
PO Box 933
Dayton, OH 45401
(800) 227–9597
www.lexis-nexis.com
(Full-text system, LEXIS concentrates on statutes and legal cases, NEXIS on business literature)

Ovid Technologies, Inc.
333 7th Avenue
New York, NY 10001
(800) 950–2035
www.ovid.com
(Concentration on education and medical databases)

Profound Business Intelligence Online
2440 W. El Camino Real
Mountain View, CA 94090
(800) 334–2564
www.profound.com
(Full text of market research reports plus general business databases)

Questel-Orbit
8000 Westpark Drive
McLean, VA 22102
(800) 456–7248
www.questel.orbit.com
(Concentration on scientific/patent databases for United States and Europe)

STN International
PO Box 3012
Columbus, OH 43210
(800) 848–6533
www.cas.org
(Concentration on scientific databases of U.S. and European origin)

Wilsonline
H.W. Wilson Co.
950 University Avenue
Bronx, NY 10452
(800) 367–6770
www.hwwilson.com
(Bibliographic databases)

APPENDIX B:
SOURCES OF BUSINESS
START-UP INFORMATION

STATE DEPARTMENTS OF LABOR

Alabama Department of Labor
100 North Union Street, Ste. 620
Montgomery, AL 36130
(334) 242–3460   alaweb.asc.edu

Alaska Department of Labor
PO Box 25501
Juneau, AK 99802
(907) 465–2700   www.state.ak.us

Arizona Department of Labor
Industrial Commission
1601 West Jefferson Street
Phoenix, AZ 85007
(602) 255–4515   www.state.az.us

Arkansas Department of Labor
10421 West Markham
Little Rock, AR 72205
(501) 682–4500   www.state.ar.us

California Department of Labor
2422 Arden Way
Sacramento, CA 95825
(916) 920–6116   www.ca.gov

Colorado Department of Labor and Employment
251 East 12th Avenue
Denver, CO 80203
(303) 620–4701   www.state.co.us

Connecticut Department of Labor
200 Folly Brook Boulevard
Wethersfield, CT 06109
(860) 566–7980   www.state.ct.us

Delaware Department of Labor
4425 Market Street
Wilmington, DE 19802
(302) 761–8000   www.state.de.us

District of Columbia Department of Employment Services
500 C Street, NW
Washington, DC 20001
(202) 639–2000   does.ci.washington.dc.us

Florida Department of Labor and Employment Security
300 Hartman Building
Tallahassee, FL 32399
(904) 488–4398   www.state.fl.us

Georgia Department of Labor
148 International Boulevard
Atlanta, GA 30303
(404) 656–3017   www.state.ga.us

Hawaii Department of Labor and Industrial Relations
830 Punchbowl Street
Honolulu, HI 96813
(808) 586–8842   www.state.hi.us

Idaho Department of Labor and Industry Service
317 Main Street
Boise, ID 93702
(208) 334–2327   www.state.id.us

Illinois Department of Labor
160 North LaSalle Street, Ste. C-1300
Chicago, IL 60601
(312) 793–2800   www.state.il.us

Indiana Division of Labor
State Office Building
Indianapolis, IN 46204
(317) 232–2655   www.state.in.us

Iowa Bureau of Labor
307 East 7th Street
Des Moines, IA 50309
(515) 281–3606   www.state.ia.us

Kansas Department of Human Resources
401 Topeka Avenue
Topeka, KS 66603
(913) 295–5000   www.state.ks.us

Kentucky Department of Labor
Capital Plaza Tower
Frankfort, KY 40601
(502) 564–3070   www.state.ky.us

Louisiana Department of Labor
PO Box 9094
Baton Rouge, LA 70804
(504) 342–3111   www.state.la.us

Maine Department of Labor
20 Union Street
Augusta, ME 04332
(207) 289–3788   www.state.me.us

Maryland Division of Labor and Industry
1 South Calvert Street
Baltimore, MD 21202
(301) 659–4180   www.state.md.us

Massachusetts Department of Labor and Industries
100 Cambridge Street
Boston, MA 02129
(617) 727–3454   www.state.ma.us

Michigan Department of Labor
Leonard Plaza
Lansing, MI 48933
(517) 373–9435   www.migov.state.mi.us

Minnesota Department of Labor and Industry
444 Lafayette Road
St. Paul, MN 55155
(612) 296–6107   www.state.mn.us

Mississippi Employment Security Commission
PO Box 1599
Jackson, MS 39215
(601) 354–8711   www.state.ms.us

Missouri Department of Labor and Industrial Relations
421 East Dunklin Street
Jefferson City, MO 65101
(573) 751–4091   www.state.mo.us

Montana Department of Labor and Industry
Labor and Industry Building
Helena, MT 59624
(406) 444–3555   www.mt.gov

Nebraska Department of Labor
550 South 16th
Lincoln, NE 68508
(402) 471–9000   www.state.ne.us

Nevada Department of Labor
505 East King Street
Carson City, NV 89701
(702) 885–4850   www.state.nv.us

New Hampshire Department of Labor
160 Manchester Street
Concord, NH 03301
(603) 271–1406   www.state.nh.us

New Jersey Department of Labor
John Fitch Plaza
Trenton, NJ 08625
(609) 292–2919   www.state.nj.us

New Mexico Department of Labor
509 Camino De Los Merquez
P.O. Box 1928
Albuquerque, NM 87103
(505) 827–2756   www.state.nm.us

New York Department of Labor
State Campus
Building 12
Albany, NY 12240
(518) 457–9000   www.state.ny.us

North Carolina Department of Labor
Labor Building
Four West Edenton Street
Raleigh, NC 27601
(919) 733–7166   www.state.nc.us

North Dakota Department of Labor
State Capitol
Bismarck, ND 58505
(701) 328–2660   www.state.nd.us

Ohio Department of Industrial Relations
2323 West 5th Avenue
Columbus, OH 43204
(614) 481–3685   www.state.oh.us

Oklahoma Department of Labor
State Capitol
Oklahoma City, OK 73105
(405) 528–5751   www.state.ok.us

Oregon Bureau of Labor
Labor and Industry Building
Portland, OR 97232
(503) 731–4070   www.state.or.us

Pennsylvania Department of Labor and Industry
Labor and Industry Building
Harrisburg, PA 17120
(717) 787–5279   www.state.pa.us

Rhode Island Department of Labor
220 Elmwood Avenue
Providence, RI 02907
(401) 277–2741   www.state.ri.us

South Carolina Department of Labor
P.O. Box 11329
Columbia, SC 29211
(803) 896–4553   www.state.sc.us

South Dakota Department of Labor
Kneip Building
Pierre, SD 57501
(605) 773–3101   www.state.sd.us

Tennessee Department of Labor
710 James Robertson Parkway
Nashville, TN 37243
(615) 741–2582   www.state.tn.us

Texas Department of Labor and Standards
Thompson State Office Building
Austin, TX 78701
(512) 475–0641   www.state.tx.us

Utah Industry and Labor Commission
350 East 500 South Street
Salt Lake City, UT 84111
(801) 530–6801   www.state.ut.us

Vermont Department of Labor and Industry
National Life Building
Montpelier, VT 05620
(802) 828–2288   www.state.vt.us

Virginia Department of Labor and Industry
Fourth Street Office Building
Richmond, VA 23261
(804) 786–2376   www.state.va.us

Washington Department of Labor and Industries
General Administration Building, Box 44000
Olympia, WA 98504
(360) 902–5800   www.wa.gov

West Virginia Department of Labor
State Office Building
Charleston, WV 25305
(304) 348–7890   www.state.wv.us

Wisconsin Department of Industry
Labor and Human Relations
PO Box 7946
Madison, WI 53707
(608) 266–3131   www.state.wi.us

Wyoming Department of Labor and Statistics
Herschler Building
Cheyenne, WY 82002
(307) 777–7261   www.state.wy.us

APPENDIX C: SAMPLE NONDISCLOSURE AGREEMENT

[Employee name], hereinafter Employee, during the term of employment, may have access to, and become familiar with, various trade secrets, inventions, formulas, devices, processes and compilations of information, records, and specifications owned by

[Company name], hereinafter Company, or its subsidiaries or entities and regularly used in the operation of the business of the Company's family of enterprises. Employee agrees not to disclose any such trade secrets, directly or indirectly, nor use them in any way, either during the term of employment, or at any time thereafter, except as required in the course of employment. All files, records, documents, drawings, specifications, equipment, and similar items relating to the business of Company, shall remain the exclusive property of Company, and shall not be removed from the premises of Company, under any circumstances, without the prior written consent of Company.

Employee agrees to hold Company harmless against any claims or actions arising from Employee's failure to maintain confidentiality.

On the termination of employment, or whenever requested by Company, the Employee shall immediately deliver to Company all property in the Employee's possession or under the Employee's control, belonging to Company, in good condition, ordinary wear, tear, and depreciation alone excepted.

Employee:_____

Date:_____

APPENDIX D: CODES OF ETHICS

AMERICAN LIBRARY ASSOCIATION CODE OF ETHICS

I. We provide the highest level of service to all library users through appropriate and usefully organized resources; equitable service policies; equitable access; and accurate, unbiased, and courteous responses to all requests.

II. We resist all efforts by groups or individuals to censor library resources or to compromise the principles of intellectual freedom.

III. We protect each library user's right to privacy with respect to information sought or received and resources consulted, borrowed, or acquired.

IV. We recognize and respect intellectual property rights.

V. We treat co-workers and other colleagues with respect, fairness, and good faith, and advocate conditions of employment that safeguard the rights and welfare of all employees of our institutions.

VI. We strive for excellence in the profession by maintaining and enhancing our own knowledge and skills, by encouraging the professional development of co-workers, and by fostering the aspirations of potential members of the profession.

VII. We do not advance private interests at the expense of library users, colleagues, or our employing institutions.

VIII. We distinguish between our professional duties and personal convictions and do not allow our personal beliefs to interfere with fair representation of the aims of our institutions or the provision of access to their information resources.

Approved by the ALA Council, June 28, 1995

AMERICAN SOCIETY FOR INFORMATION SCIENCE (ASIS) PROFESSIONAL GUIDELINES

RESPONSIBILITIES TO EMPLOYERS/CLIENTS/SYSTEM USERS

To act faithfully for their employers or clients in professional matters.

To uphold each user's, provider's, or employer's right to privacy and confidentiality and to respect whatever proprietary rights belong to them, by

limiting access to, providing proper security for and ensuring proper disposal of data about clients, patrons or users.

RESPONSIBILITY TO THE PROFESSION

To truthfully represent themselves and the information systems which they utilize or which they represent, by

not knowingly making false statements or providing erroneous or misleading information

informing their employers, clients or sponsors of any circumstances that create a conflict of interest

not using their position beyond their authorized limits or by not using their credentials to misrepresent themselves

following and promoting standards of conduct in accord with the best current practices

undertaking their research conscientiously, in gathering, tabulating or interpreting data; in following proper approval procedures for subjects; and in producing or disseminating their research results

pursuing ongoing professional development and encouraging and assisting colleagues and others to do the same

adhering to principles of due process and equality of opportunity.

RESPONSIBILITY TO SOCIETY

To improve the information systems with which they work or which they represent, to the best of their means and abilities by providing the most reliable and accurate information and acknowledging the credibility of the sources as known or unknown

resisting all forms of censorship, inappropriate selection and acquisitions policies, and bias in information selection, provision and dissemination

making known any bias, errors or inaccuracies found to exist and striving to correct those which can be remedied.

To promote open and equal access to information, within the scope permitted by their organizations or work, and to resist procedures that promote unlawful discriminatory practices in access to and provision of information, by

seeking to extend public awareness and appreciation of information availability and provision as well as the role of information professionals in providing such information

freely reporting, publishing or disseminating information subject to legal and proprietary restraints of producers, vendors and employers, and the best interests of their employers or clients

Information professionals shall engage in principled conduct whether on their own behalf or at the request of employers, colleagues, clients, agencies or the profession.

Approved by the ASIS Board, 1993.

AIIP [ASSOCIATION OF INDEPENDENT INFORMATION PROFESSIONALS] CODE OF ETHICAL BUSINESS PRACTICE

An Independent Information Professional is an entrepreneur who has demonstrated continuing expertise in the art of finding and organizing information. Each provides information services on a contractual basis to more than one client and serves as an objective intermediary between the client and the information world.

An Information Professional bears the following responsibilities:

1. Uphold the profession's reputation for honesty, competence, and confidentiality.

2. Give clients the most current and accurate information possible within the budget and time frames provided by the client.
3. Help clients understand the sources of information used and the degree of reliability which can be expected.
4. Accept only those projects which are legal and are not detrimental to our profession.
5. Respect client confidentiality as requested or required by clients, including nature of the services provided, identity of the clients, and subject matter of work performed.
6. Recognize intellectual property rights, licensing agreements and other contractual agreements with vendors, and to explain to clients what their obligations may be to these agreements.
7. Maintain a professional relationship with libraries and comply with all their rules of access.
8. Assume responsibility for employees' compliance with this code.

Approved by the membership May 5, 1989, at the Third National Conference and Annual Meeting in Lowell, Massachusetts.

Amended by the membership April 22, 1990, at the Fourth National Conference and Annual Meeting in San Francisco, California.

Amended by the membership April 18, 1997, at the Eleventh National Conference and Annual Meeting in Orlando, Florida.

ACM [ASSOCIATION FOR COMPUTING MACHINERY] CODE OF ETHICS AND PROFESSIONAL CONDUCT

As an ACM member I will . . .

1.1   Contribute to society and human well being.
1.2   Avoid harm to others.
1.3   Be honest and trustworthy.
1.4   Be fair and take action not to discriminate.
1.5   Honor property rights including copyrights and patents.
1.6   Give proper credit for intellectual property.
1.7   Respect the privacy of others.
1.8   Honor confidentiality.

As an ACM computing professional, I will . . .

2.1 Strive to achieve the highest quality, effectiveness and dignity in both the process and products of professional work.
2.2 Acquire and maintain professional competence.
2.3 Know and respect existing laws pertaining to professional work.
2.4 Accept and provide appropriate professional review.
2.5 Give comprehensive and thorough evaluations of computer systems and their impacts, including analysis of possible risks.
2.6 Honor contracts, agreements and assigned responsibilities.
2.7 Improve public understanding of computing and its consequences.
2.8 Access computing and communication resources only when authorized to do so.

As an ACM member and an organizational leader, I will . . .

3.1 Articulate social responsibilities of members of an organizational unit and encourage full acceptance of those responsibilities.
3.2 Manage personnel and resources to design and build information systems that enhance the quality of working life.
3.3 Acknowledge and support proper and authorized uses of an organization's computing and communication resources.
3.4 Ensure that users and those who will be affected by a system have their needs clearly articulated during the assessment and design of requirements. Later the system must be validated to meet requirements.
3.5 Articulate and support policies that protect the dignity of users and others affected by a computing system.
3.6 Create opportunities for members of the organization to learn the principles and limitations of computer systems.

As a ACM member I will . . .

4.1 Uphold and promote the principles of the code.
4.2 Treat violations of this code as inconsistent with membership in the ACM.

Adopted by the Association for Computing Machinery's Executive Council on October 16, 1992. From "The New ACM Code of Ethics in Decision Making," *Communications of the ACM*, 1993, 1–6.

BASIC BUSINESS REFERENCE SOURCES

Bureau of the Census. *Census Catalog and Guide*, which includes information on everything the bureau collects and has available, including all prices for reports. If your public library doesn't have it, you can order it from the Government Printing Office, Superintendent of Documents, PO Box 371954, Pittsburgh, PA 15250, (202) 512–1800.

———.*The Census Bureau's State and Metropolitan Area Data Book*, which offers demographic and economic facts and figures by region, or the *County and City Data Book*. You can order either book from the Superintendent of Documents (see above).

———. *Statistical Abstract of the United States*. Washington, DC: Government Printing Office, annual.

Columbia University Press. *The New Columbia Encyclopedia* (one volume). New York, Columbia University Press, latest edition.

Monroe, K.M., et al. *Secretary's Handbook*. 9th ed. New York: Macmillan, 1969. Note: If unavailable in the local bookstore, any similar title will probably serve as well.

Office of the Federal Register. National Archives and Records Administration. *United States Government Manual*. Washington, DC; biannual.

Roget's Thesaurus in Dictionary Form. Available in hard or soft cover.

United States Postal Service. *1986 National ZIP Code and Post Office Directory*. Can be purchased at many post offices or by mail from Information Center, 6060 Primacy Parkway, Suite 101, Memphis, TN 38188. Note: Smaller ZIP directories are available at some bookstores and may be sufficient for the average business needs.

Webster's New Collegiate Dictionary. Springfield, MA: G. & C. Merriam Company, latest edition.

World Almanac and Book of Facts. New York: Pharos Books, annual.

ADDITIONAL RESOURCES

CHAPTER 1: BECOMING AN INFORMATION BROKER

Basch, Reva. "Information Brokers as Consultants." *Information Today* (January 1992): 9–11.

———. "The Seven Deadly Sins of Full-Text Searching." *Database* (August 1989): 15–23.

Edwards, Sarah, and Paul Edwards. *Secrets of Self-Employment.* Putnam, 1996.

Everett, John, and Elizabeth Crowe. *Information for Sale.* 2d ed. Wincrest/McGraw-Hill, 1994.

"Information Brokering." *Bulletin of the American Society for Information Science* 21 (3) (February/March 1995).

Mount, Ellis (ed.) "Fee-based Services in Sci-Tech Libraries." *Science and Technology Libraries* 5 (2) (1984).

Rugge, Sue, and Alfred Glossbrenner. *The Information Broker's Handbook.* 3d ed. Computing McGraw-Hill, 1997.

Warner, Alice Sizer. *Mind Your Own Business: A Guide for the Information Entrepreneur.* Neal-Schuman, 1987.

Woodsworth, Anne, and James Williams. *Managing the Economics of Owning, Leasing and Contracting Out Information Services.* Ashgate, 1993.

CHAPTER 2: DEVELOPING YOUR SERVICE DELIVERY STRATEGY

Badaracco, Joseph L. *The Knowledge Link: How Firms Compete Through Strategic Alliances.* Harvard Business School Press, 1991.

Basch, Reva. *Secrets of the Super Net Searchers.* Pemberton Press, 1996.

———. *Secrets of the Super Searchers.* Online, 1993.

Bates, Mary Ellen. "Finding Full-Text Market Research." *Database* (August 1993): 30.

———. *The Online Deskbook: Online Magazine's Essential Desk Reference for Online and Internet Searchers.* Pemberton, 1996.

Culligan, Joseph. *You Too, Can Find Anybody: A Reference Manual.* Hallmark Press, 1991.

Eells, Richard and Peter Nehemkis. *Corporate Intelligence and Espionage.* Macmillan, 1984.

Elias, Stephen, and Kate McGrath. *Trademark: How to Name Your Business and Product.* Nolo Press, 1992.

Ernst, Douglas. "Academic Libraries, Fee-Based Information Services, and the Business Community." *RQ* 32 (1993): 393–402.

Fuld, Leonard. *Competitor Intelligence.* 2d ed. John Wiley, 1994.

Fulltext Sources Online. BiblioData. Published semiannually.

Gale Directory of Databases. Gale Research. Published semiannually.

Greene, H. Frances. "Competitive Intelligence and the Information Center." *Special Libraries* 79 (4) (Fall 1988): 285–294.

Guide to Background Investigations. National Employment Screening Services, 1993.

"How to Protect and Benefit from Your Ideas." The American Intellectual Property Law Association (AIPLA), 2001 Jefferson Davis Highway, Suite 203, Arlington, VA 22202.

Information Plus America. "Tradecraft Newsletter: The Sourcebook of Competitive Intelligence Tactics." Information Plus (America) Inc., 14 Lafayette Square, Suite 2000, Buffalo, NY 14203, (716) 852–2220. $115.00 annually.

King, Dennis. *Get the Facts on Anyone.* Simon & Schuster, 1992.

Lane, Carole A. *Naked in Cyberspace.* Pemberton Press, 1996.

Lesko, Matthew. *The Federal Database Finder.* Information USA, 1990.

Prusak, Laurence. *Knowledge in Organizations.* Butterworth-Heinemann, 1997.

The Reporter's Handbook. St. Martin's Press, 1990.

Superintendent of Documents, "General Information Concerning Patents." U.S. Government Printing Office, PO Box, 371954, Pittsburgh, PA 15250; $2.25 (202) 512–1800.

Tenopir, Carol, and Jung Soon Ro. *Fulltext Databases.* Greenwood Press, 1990.

Thomas, Ralph. *Business Intelligence Investigations.* Thomas Publications, 1991.

U.S. Patent and Trademark Office. "Basic Facts About Trademarks." Department of Commerce, Commissioner of Patents and Trademarks, U.S. Patent and Trademark Office, Washington, DC 20231; free; (703) 308–9000.

Von Krogh, Georg, and Johan Roos. *Managing Knowledge: Perspectives on Cooperation and Competition.* Sage, 1996.

Weinstein, David. *How to Protect Your Business, Professional, and Brand Names.* John Wiley, 1990.

CHAPTER 3: STARTING YOUR OWN FIRM

Abrams, Rhonda M. *The Successful Business Plan*. Oasis, 1993.

Bangs, David H., Jr. *The Business Planning Guide*. Upstart, 1996.

Burton, E. James. *Total Business Planning*. John Wiley, 1991.

Gumpert, David E. *How to Really Create a Successful Business Plan*. Inc. Pub., 1996.

Hopson, James. "Helping Clients Choose the Legal Form for a Small Business." *The Practical Accountant* (October 1990): 67–70, 78–84.

Hotch, Ripley. *How to Start a Business and Succeed*. Stackpole Books, 1991.

Jehle, Faustin, E. *Complete and Easy Guide to Social Security and Medicare*. Fraser, 1997.

Kennedy, Dan S. *Getting Ready*. Self Counsel Press, 1991.

———. *Getting Started*. Self Counsel Press, 1991.

Kravitt, Gregory. *Creating a Winning Business Plan*. Joraco, 1992.

Kuehl, Charles, and Peggy Lambing. *Small Business Planning and Management*. 2d ed. Dryden Press, 1990.

Luther, William M. *The Start-Up Business Plan*. Macmillan, 1991.

Mazzo, William L. *A Business Plan and Evaluation*. Business Plan Publishing, 1991.

McGarty, Terrence P. *Business Plans that Win Venture Capital*. John Wiley, 1990.

McKeever, Mike P. *How to Write a Business Plan*. Nolo Press, 1993.

McLaughlin, Harold J. *The Entrepreneur's Guide to Building a Better Business Plan*. John Wiley, 1992.

O'Donnell, Michael. *Writing Business Plans that Get Results*. Contemporary Books, 1991.

O'Hara, Patrick D. *The Total Business Plan*. John Wiley, 1994.

Schilit, W. Keith. *The Entrepreneur's Guide to Preparing a Winning Business Plan and Raising Venture Capital*. Prentice Hall, 1990.

Silver, David. *Up Front Financing: The Entrepreneur's Guide*. John Wiley, 1988.

CHAPTER 4: MANAGING YOUR PRACTICE

Brown, Yvette. "From the Reference Desk to the Jail House: Unauthorized Practice of Law and Librarians." *Legal Reference Services Quarterly* 13 (4) (Winter 1994): 31–45.

Denis, Sabine, and Yves Pouliet. "Questions of Liability in the Provision of Information Services." *Online Review* 14 (1) (1990): 21–32.

Dragich, Martha J. "Information Malpractice: Some Thoughts on the Potential Liability of Information Professionals." *Information Technology & Libraries* 8 (3) (September 1989): 265–272.

Dun & Bradstreet v. Greenmoss Builders, Inc., 105 S.Ct. 2939 (1985).

Edmonds, Diana. "The Information Product: Is the Broker Liable for Giving the Wrong Answer?" *Infomediary* 4 (3/4)(1990): 121–126.

Nasri, William Z. "Professional Liability." *Journal of Library Administration* 7 (4) (Winter 1986): 141–145.

Steingold, Fred. *The Legal Guide for Starting and Running a Small Business.* Nolo Press, 1993.

Tomaiuolo, Nicholas G., and Barbara J. Frey. "Computer Database Searching and Professional Malpractice: Who Cares?" *Bulletin of the Medical Library Association* 80 (4) (October 1992): 367–370.

Uniform Commercial Code, Sections 2–102, 2–105(1) and (2), 2–313, 2–314, 2–315, 2–316, 2–317.

Williams, Wilda. "Malpractice Issues in Librarianship." *Library Journal* 117 (19) (November 15, 1992): 64.

CHAPTER 5: BILLING FOR SERVICES

Bates, Mary Ellen. "Cost Control: Using Automatic Accounting Features to Monitor Search Costs." *Online* 17 (January 1993): 39–43.

Shenson, Howard. *Shenson on Consulting.* John Wiley, 1994.

———. *The Contract and Fee Setting Guide for Consultants and Professionals.* John Wiley, 1990.

CHAPTER 6: WORKING WITH CLIENTS

Buschman, John. "Critique of the Information Broker: Contexts of Reference Services." *Reference Librarian* 31 (1990): 131–151.

Henderson, Fiona. "The Client's View of Information Brokers." *Infomediary* (December 1990): 127–134.

Quint, Barbara. "Inside a Searcher's Mind: The Seven Stages of an Online Search." *Online* 15 (May 1991): 13–18.

Rosen, Linda. "The Information Professional as Knowledge Engineer." *Information Today* (May 1993).

CHAPTER 7: MARKETING YOUR BUSINESS

Carlson, Linda. *The Publicity and Promotion Handbook: A Complete Guide for Small Business*. Van Nostrand Reinhold, 1982.

Cronin, Mary. *Doing More Business on the Internet*. Van Nostrand Reinhold, 1995.

Edwards, Paul, Sarah Edwards and Laura Clampitt Douglas. *Getting Business to Come to You*. Jeremy Tarcher, 1991.

Ellsworth, Jill, and Matthew Ellsworth. *Marketing on the Internet*. John Wiley, 1995.

———. *The Internet Business Book*. John Wiley, 1994.

Janel, Daniel. *Online Marketing Handbook: How to Sell, Advertise, Publicize and Promote Your Products and Services on the Internet and Commercial Online Systems*. Van Nostrand Reinhold, 1995.

Levinson, Jay Conrad, and Seth Godin. *Guerrilla Marketing for the Home-Based Business*. Houghton Mifflin, 1995.

O'Connor, Dick, and Jeffrey Davidson. *Marketing Your Consulting and Professional Services*. John Wiley, 1990.

Phillips, Michael, and Salli Rasberry. *Marketing without Advertising*. Nolo Press. 1992.

Resnick, Rosalind, and Dave Taylor. *Internet Business Guide*. 2d ed. Sams.net Publishing, 1995

CHAPTER 8: THE RESPONSIBLE BROKER

Anderson, Ronald, Deborah Johnson, Donald Gotterbarn, and Judith Perrolle. "Using the New ACM Code of Ethics in Decision Making." *Communications of the ACM* 1993.

Branscomb, Anne. *Who Owns Information?* Basic Books, 1994.

Cooper, Terry. *The Responsible Administrator*. Jossey-Bass, 1990.

Cronin, Blaise, and Elisabeth Davenport. *Post-professionalism: Transforming the Information Heartland*. Taylor Graham, 1988.

Crowe, Lawson, and Susan Anthes. "The Academic Librarian and Information Technology: Ethical Issues." *College and Research Libraries* 49 (March 1988): 123–130.

The Information Advisor Newsletter. Available from Information Advisory Services, Inc., 47 Wilmer Street, Rochester, New York.

Larson, Erik. *The Naked Consumer*. Henry Holt, 1992.

Laudon, Kenneth. *The Dossier Society*. Columbia University Press, 1986.

Lewis, Carol. *The Ethics Challenge in Public Service.* Jossey-Bass, 1991.

Lindsey, Jonathan, and Ann Prentice. *Professional Ethics and Librarians.* Oryx, 1985.

Mintz, Anne. "Ethics and the News Librarian." *Special Libraries* 82 (1) (Winter 1991): 7–11.

———, "Information Practice and Malpractice: Do We Need Malpractice Insurance?" *Online* 8 (4) (July 1984): 20–26.

———, ed. *Information Ethics: Concerns for Librarianship and the Information Industry.* McFarland, 1990.

Nock, Steven. *The Costs of Privacy.* DeGruyter, 1993.

Rothfeder, Jeffrey. *Privacy for Sale.* Simon & Schuster, 1992.

Swan, John. "Ethics Inside and Out." *Library Trends* 40 (2) (Fall 1991): 259–274.

Westin, A.F. *Privacy and Freedom.* Atheneum, 1967.

INDEX

ABOUT THE AUTHORS

Florence Mason is owner and principal of F. Mason and Associates, a consulting firm in Dallas that specializes in library and information management issues. Before becoming a library management consultant, she owned a number of small businesses, including retail businesses, a bicycle shop, and a tour firm specializing in tour packages. She was also a senior consultant for HBW Associates, a library planning and consulting firm in Dallas. She is an adjunct professor in the Schools of Library and Information Science for the University of North Texas and Emporia State University and has taught graduate courses in information brokering and information service design. Mason's MLS is from Simmons College.

Chris Dobson is president and founder of F1 Services, Inc., an information brokering firm founded in 1988. F1 Services, based in Dallas, provides services to corporate and private industry clients. As an active charter member of the Association of Independent Information Professionals, she has advised many individuals who were starting and operating their own businesses. Over the past three years she has taught adult education courses on information brokering for Fun Ed, a continuing education provider in Dallas. Before founding F1 Services, she held library positions with American Airlines, Core Laboratories, and Infomart in Dallas. Dobson holds an MLS from Texas Woman's University.